# Divorce and Beyond

## *A Workbook for Recovery and Healing*

**James Greteman**
**Leon Haverkamp**

Revised by
**Elsie P. Radtke**

**ACTA**
**ASSISTING CHRISTIANS TO ACT**
PUBLICATIONS

***Divorce and Beyond***
***A Workbook for Recovery and Healing***
by James Greteman, CSC, and Leon Havercamp, MSW
revised by Elsie P. Radtke

Edited by Todd J. Behme and Gregory F. Augustine Pierce
Cover design by Tom A. Wright
Typesetting by Desktop Edit Shop, Inc.
Cover photo used under rights granted to Seescapes Publishing

Excerpts and adaptations from the following books were used
with permission:
*Creative Divorce* by M. Krantzler (New American Library, 1973)
*Divorce and After* by P. Bohannon (Doubleday, 1971)
*Growing through Divorce* by J. Smoke (Harvest House Publishers, 1976)
*Help It All Makes Sense, Lord!* by E. Witt (Concordia Publishing
    House, 1972)
*How to Get Angry without Feeling Guilty* by A. Bry (Signet Books, 1976)
*Mom's House, Dad's House* by I. Ricci (McMillan Publishing Co., 1980)
*The Pain of Being Human* by E. Kennedy (Image Books, 1972)
*Psycho-Cybernetics* by M. Maltz (Prentice-Hall, Inc., 1969)
*Rebel, O Jews!* by M. Fisher (Reconstructionist Press, 1973)
*The Social Readjustment Rating Scale* by T. Holmes and R. Rahe
    (Journal of Psychosomatic Research, Vol. II, 1967)
*Traits of a Healthy Spirituality* by M. Svoboda (Twenty-Third
    Publications, 1996)

Copyright © 1983, 2004 by: ACTA Publications
                    Assisting Christians To Act
                    4848 N. Clark Street
                    Chicago, IL 60640-4711
                    773-271-1030
                    www.actapublications.com

Library of Congress Card Number: 2004092242
ISBN: 0-915388-16-2
Printed in the United States of America
Year: 10 09 08 07 06 05 04
Printing: 10 9 8 7 6 5 4 3 2 1

# Contents

# Appendices

# Foreword

For a tree there is always hope.
Chop it down and it still has a chance—
Its roots can put out fresh sprouts.
Even if its roots are old and gnarled,
Its stump long dormant,
At the first whiff of water it comes to life,
Buds and grows like a sapling.

*Job 14:7-9*

One of the greatest mysteries of life is that both suffering and joy often come completely unforeseen. For those of us who marry, for example, we seldom do so with the expectation that one day our marriage will end. We are confident we will be able to work out whatever differences and conflicts may arise. Too often we are sadly disillusioned. I can recall myself in the first years of marriage thinking: "What's wrong with those people who are getting divorced? Why don't they just work it out? They loved each other enough to commit to one another, yet now they are divorcing." Yet after eighteen years of marriage and four children, I found that my own marriage was ending. I was one of "them."

Divorce does not happen in a courtroom. It begins long before two people decide they can't work it out or one of the partners decides to leave. And the process, or the uncoupling, usually continues long after the judge issues the decree. This is why I use the term "divorcing"—to emphasize the process. A legal decree does not automatically bring emotional and psychological divorce. We are truly divorced only when we finally let go of our marriage, mourn our loss, and adjust ourselves to our new life. At the end of this process, it is not unusual for people to feel stronger and happier than ever before. What started out as the worst experience in the world transforms into a blessing of life. But this occurs only when we do the work that needs to be done.

Perhaps the best teachers of what is involved in this work are other people who have gone or are going through a divorce. Participants in divorce recovery programs such as *Divorce and Beyond* commonly ex-

5

perience hope and healing simply by listening and sharing experiences and insights with others who are able to avoid giving advice and pronouncing judgments. Even if you are seeing a therapist one-on-one, a group setting can help you by showing you that others are experiencing similar feelings. You are not alone in this experience. This program is an opportunity to build a network of friends who accept where you are at this point in your life.

Many of us divorced people often feel guilt and shame at not being able to keep our marriage intact. We may feel a sense of failure in not living out our wedding vows, and for many of us it is painful to see other families together in church, to the point where we avoid going to church ourselves. But divorce does not mean we are not holy or worthy of God's love. We are still a part of our own family and the family that is the Church, even if we are living alone or with our young children. As you continue through this program, take advantage of the sacraments frequently, and spend time in prayer. Ponder Christ's life. He knows what it means to be human. Your strength will come from him.

I have spent sixteen years working with divorced and divorcing people, leading many groups through this book. I am confident that this revised version of *Divorce and Beyond* will be a helpful guide for you, allowing you to apply to your own life the graces earned by the death and resurrection of Jesus Christ and helping you view the end of your marriage as God's calling to discover the person he created you to be.

*Irene Varley*
*Executive Director*
*North American Conference of Separated and Divorced Catholics*

# Introduction

Divorce *is* painful, often shatteringly so. I know because I have been through it myself. Though the trauma is intense, divorce need not be the end of our productive and fulfilling life. It becomes an unmitigated tragedy only if we fail to learn something from it about ourselves and about relationships.

Even as we grow from our divorce, however, it still causes much grief. Here are some general truths about grief to consider, adapted from *The New Day Journal* by Sr. Mauryeen O'Brien:

- Grief is a normal and natural reaction to any significant loss.
- Few of us are prepared for the long journey of grief.
- No two people grieve the same way.
- In order to move beyond your grief you must work at it; there is no alternative.
- It is not selfish to be self-caring.
- Grief work takes much longer than most people expect.
- The best therapy for grief is to find people who will listen to your "grief story" over and over.

All of us grow by recognizing and responding to the call of God that comes to us in the events of our everyday lives—things as mundane as washing the dishes, as exhilarating as becoming a parent, and as painful as divorcing. But because divorce changes so many aspects of our life, including our spiritual life, many of us find that we need the special comfort and insight that can be found only in a group of people who are experiencing similar pain and suffering.

That is what *Divorce and Beyond* is really all about and why I am honored to have been asked to revise this wonderful program, originally written by Leon Haverkamp and my friend Brother James Greteman.

*Divorce and Beyond* is for people who are already divorced or have filed for divorce. It examines what happens to most husbands and

7

wives going through the breakup of their marriage. It helps participants understand what they are going through and that others have gone through the same things. Finally, it suggests activities for making divorce a growth experience.

The program asks that you commit yourself to all the sessions. You and the other participants will share insights you gain from reflecting on your experiences and the reading material and exercises. The readings and exercises do not by any means attempt to cover all the important information about each topic; they are intended to start you thinking and to help you organize your thoughts. Similarly, the sessions will not attempt to summarize or analyze; therefore, you are again encouraged to take an active role by writing down the things you want to remember.

This book was originally written for Catholics, and this revision has not altered that intent. In my many years of Catholic divorce ministry, however, I know that people of many faiths have benefit from attending the small groups of *Divorce and Beyond*. So please feel free to adapt this book to suit your situation. Divorce is painful for all of us, and how God works through each of us is how we heal. Don't let the rubrics of religion deny you the benefit of shared growth.

A final note of encouragement: Although Jesus called his disciples to follow him to perfection, he never ceased to love them in their imperfect humanity. He called them to strive for wholeness, but he did not turn his back on them when they failed or were afraid. He understood that performance seldom measures up to its promise.

So it is with those of us who are divorced.

**Elsie P. Radtke**
*Associate Director*
*Coordinator of Divorce and Annulment Support Ministries*
*Family Ministries Office*
*Archdiocese of Chicago*

# Session One
# The Process of Divorce

---

### Before We Begin
Respond to the three questions below in writing. A sentence or two for each is sufficient.

What do you want your life to be like in a year?
What do you hope to get out of this *Divorce and Beyond* program?
What does the ending of your marriage represent to you at this time?

After you write your answers, put your paper into an envelope, seal it and put your name on the envelope and hand it to the facilitator. It will be kept safe and confidential until later in the program, and no one else will ever see your responses.

---

## Reflection
Divorce is a process, not simply a legal decree. This process has often been compared to a journey across a bridge. On one side of the bridge is the broken relationship, with all the feelings of failure and hopelessness that result. On the other side is a balanced life, where people have accepted the past and eagerly await the future. The bridge itself, however, is a rickety contrivance of ropes and irregularly spaced boards. As travelers gingerly grope their way across, they feel the fragmentation, fear and confusion that attend any journey past unknown risks toward an unknown destination. Understanding the three basic stages of divorce will help you go through the process with the hope of finally being able to say, "The past is dead, and I'm ready for a new and better life."

### Stage 1: The Death of the Relationship
Divorce happens in two ways. In about ten percent of the cases it is a "sudden death"—for example, one spouse comes home and announces out of the blue that he or she is leaving. However, in most

cases divorce is a lingering death that extends over many months or even years. Usually the relationship has died long before the couple or one of the partners files for divorce.

Marriages end up in divorce courts for widely varying reasons, but one common theme is couples' difficulty in communicating to each other what they expected the marriage relationship to provide for themselves and their partners. It is impossible to sum up the complex relationship between two people who live intimately with each other, but there are some basic needs that all spouses expect their marriage to fulfill.

The most basic need in every marriage is pure survival. Both partners need food, shelter and clothing. Because this is obvious, couples seldom have problems communicating this need to each other. (What they do about it is another matter, however.) Less understood, and often very difficult to communicate, is the degree to which spouses expect their partners to recognize and fulfill the following needs:

- **Physical**. To be physically close, to touch, to hug and be hugged, and to be sexually involved with their partner.
- **Emotional**. To feel special and important, and to feel freedom to express their love to their partner.
- **Intellectual**. To communicate their own ideas and opinions; to solve problems, make plans and set goals together.
- **Spiritual**. To recognize and accept the faith experiences and dimensions of the other, and to share common values.

As you review the story of your marriage and remember critical episodes, you may find that one or more of these needs were not being met for you or your partner. You also may realize that by expecting marriage to meet all your needs all the time, you or your partner may have placed an impossible burden on your relationship.

Many couples reflecting on their courtship and early married life remember how easily they related physically and emotionally. This often is enough to keep couples happy and satisfied in the beginning. However, when the glow and excitement that are part of early marriage begin to diminish, partners begin to feel the need to relate on deeper intellectual and spiritual levels. If this happens for both partners at the same time, chances are that they will grow together in love, respect and trust. If they agree on the fundamentals of how they will live—intellectually and spiritually—their union will be stable. This assumes, of course, that they are flexible enough to allow themselves and their partners the freedom to share these vital areas of their lives with others too.

Trouble often comes when one spouse expects the other to become deeply involved in things in which the latter finds it difficult or impossible to participate—such as hobbies, church activities, or even raising the children. When one partner is not able or willing to share and communicate to the degree that the other expects, both may begin building barriers of hurt and misunderstanding. Their warm, positive feelings for each other slowly transform into negative ones, and they begin moving apart. With the loss of closeness, real sexual intimacy becomes increasingly difficult, and their sexual relations may deteriorate into a routine, an obligation, or a weapon. Finally one or both of the partners begin to withdraw, and the relationship has begun to die. This dying process may go on for years before a couple recognizes it and files for divorce.

## Stage 2: The Mourning Period

Whatever the reasons for it or however long it took in coming, a divorce results in feelings of pain, anger, failure, rejection and even helplessness. Some of us initially feel euphoric about our divorce—happy to be free from a bad situation and out of a dysfunctional relationship. But such positive feelings seldom last long, and sooner or later they are replaced by negative ones. This holds true no matter who initiated the divorce.

Two behavior patterns, denial and bargaining, characterize the "mourning period" of divorce. At first many of us deny that our marriage is really over. We feel numb and shocked. We find it hard to admit to ourselves that our spouse will not return, and harder yet to admit this to others. Pretending and fantasizing become a habit, and we are tempted to deny any responsibility for the death of the relationship.

The second pattern is bargaining. Sometimes we even offer to do or become anything our ex-partner might want just to make things go back to the way they were. We offer to change our ways, and we begin the old "I wonder what would happen if I ..." game. The loneliness and unhappiness we are experiencing seem too high a price to pay for freedom from a bad relationship.

It takes most of us a long time, perhaps nine to twelve months, to go through the mourning period of divorce. This is a very important time, however, for during this period we deal with feelings that we must acknowledge and accept. What we are mourning is the death of a very important relationship—the loss of our companion, lover, friend, home, financial security, familiar role and most of all our future, which we once considered settled and secure. With these losses come the painful emotions that are an integral part of grief. Some of

11

these emotions—such as anger, guilt, anxiety, tension and loneliness—will be dealt with later in this program.

Mourning is a difficult stage of divorce. There is no escaping it, no shortcuts, no easy answers. In fact, the greater your past commitment to the marriage was, the more difficult the mourning phase will be. The end will come only when you accept your former marriage as a part of the past that cannot be changed; when you view your former partner as someone who cannot and should not control you or be controlled by you any longer; and, finally, when you recognize that you must build a new life as a newly single person.

A very important part of this "letting go" is understanding that only the *relationship* has failed. You and your former spouse are not failures. You are still alive and functioning, and you both have the potential to make other relationships work.

## Stage 3: Regaining Balance

Sometimes it takes us years to regain our balance after the divorce. We have to decide who we are if we can no longer identify ourselves as one half of "Mr. and Mrs. Right." We must decide where we want to go and what we want to do with the rest of our lives. We need to acquire a new understanding and acceptance of ourselves in order to feel comfortable in our new role as a single person and perhaps a single parent. We might need to learn new practical skills. This is a difficult but exciting challenge. It will include finding new and better ways of relating to people on all levels. It will mean opening doors to new experiences and new people.

The stages of death, mourning and regaining balance in our lives will overlap. For example, some of us who are well into a comfortable pattern as a single person will suddenly find ourselves calling our former husband or wife for superficial reasons. This two-steps-forward-one-step-back behavior is to be expected. No process is as linear as it appears on paper, but overall we can move forward. The journey across the bridge of divorce does not have an end in the same way it began. Patience and gentleness is required for those of us who want to cross this bridge successfully.

## Exercise One
*Write your responses in the back of your notebook.*

1. When you first realized your marriage was over, what were some of your feelings? (To help get you started, here are some possible words to use: angry, fearful, rejected, abandoned, free, guilty, sad, isolated, diminished, relieved, anxious, victimized, challenged.)
2. How have your feelings changed since your marriage ended?

## Exercise Two
*Read the following and discuss with the group where you are in the divorce process and what things are causing you the greatest difficulty.*

In *Divorce and After: An Analysis of the Emotional and Social Problems of Divorce,* Paul Bohannon described six divorce experiences that affect peoples' daily lives. These experiences, which may come at different times or overlap, carry varying degrees of pain and frustration:

1. **Emotional Divorce:** Begins when the decision is made to divorce.
2. **Economic Divorce:** Begins when the partners set up separate residences.
3. **Legal Divorce:** Begins when a judge issues the final decree.
4. **Co-parental Divorce:** Involves assuming different parenting roles.
5. **Community Divorce:** Involves loosening ties with some old friends and acquaintances and starting new friendships.
6. **Psychic Divorce:** Involves establishing individual autonomy.

### Before the Next Session
Begin to write down the story, or account, of what happened in your divorce. True, your perception of your history will change as time passes. And because this program is based on the experience of the participants, you will be telling much of your story during the sessions. Nevertheless, you will discover a great value in writing it out for yourself. Whether your version at this time is factually accurate or not, whether it is made up of insights or excuses, you will find that developing your story as you see it now is a vital tool for coping with self-doubt and guilt.

Before the group meets next time, begin to write your story. As this program progresses, look back on your story every so often and rewrite the parts you view with a different perspective. Repeat this exercise periodically until you can finally read your story, accept it, live with it, and close the door on the past.

A simple way to organize your story is to divide part of your notebook into five manageable time segments or chapters. In your notebook label the chapters with these titles:

1. **Courtship**
2. **Years of Marriage**
3. **Breakup of Marriage**
4. **Mourning Period**
5. **Regaining Balance**

After each chapter title write the time frame of the period, such as "three years" or "1995-98." You may have nothing to write in the fifth period, Regaining Balance, but that is to be expected at this time. Leave a number of blank pages after each title page.

Each chapter should include the things you consider significant in that period (e.g., children's births, places you lived, jobs, significant illnesses). Pay particular attention to how you felt during these times (happy, sad, depressed, at peace). Each week of this program, you will add to your story as part of your Reflection Exercise.

# Coping Tips in the Divorce Process

While the mourning period will take time and work, there are things you can do to make it easier. Below are some helpful suggestions and observations. Read them over and reread them periodically. Many of these will be emphasized during the rest of the program.

- Admit your loss.
- Say out loud that you are hurting.
- Do not fantasize; allow reality to happen.
- You will experience highs and lows, like a roller-coaster ride.
- You do have a future.
- Proceed gently.
- Keep major decisions to a minimum.
- It is OK to ask for comfort.
- Look for support from a friend, a relative, the church, etc.
- Be around living things—plants and pets.
- Keep your values in focus.
- Keep in control of the days that are especially difficult (like birthdays and anniversaries) by scheduling or organizing events for yourself.
- Bad feelings do pass.
- Allow yourself to feel the hurt.
- Praying helps.
- Use a list to help structure your day.
- Feelings are neither good nor bad; it is what you do with them that counts.
- Eat in a healthy way.
- Proceed slowly.
- Take thoughtful, careful risks.
- Go easy in your use of things that may become addicting.
- Take care of yourself.
- Writing your thoughts down may help.
- Heal at your own rate.
- Exercise daily.

# Session Two
# Self-Image

## Reflection

The picture we hold of ourselves is the key to our personality and behavior. Before any self-help program can help us work through the emotions that dominate our lives, we divorced people must look at one of the strongest forces within ourselves—our self-image.

Many of us have experienced rejection and believe we have failed in a vital area of our lives—our marriage. These feelings often cause us to think of ourselves as failures, as unworthy of respect and happiness. If we don't do something to change this perception, we may begin to act like failures—and may even *become* failures.

Human beings have an instinct not only for survival but also to strive for health and happiness. Our Creator has equipped us to see options, set goals, learn new habits, and create new experiences—experiences that can help us see ourselves and our lives in new, more positive terms. Unfortunately, simply wishing for a more positive self-image will not achieve it. We have to believe in the new image in order for it to be effective. To change our self-image, we must use our imagination, our reason, and all our God-given resources in a determined effort to recognize and accept our true worth.

Bad habits are learned during or after a divorce; better habits also can be learned. A concrete program of self-affirmation can change patterns of thinking from negative to positive, but this process takes time and work. We divorced people face new experiences whether we like it or not. Simply having these experiences can give us a better way of looking at ourselves, our lives and our times. However, it is much better for us if we can be open to new things, ideas, people and events, and perhaps even plan for them. Setting and reaching new goals brings a real sense of achievement and growth.

You can achieve a better, more positive self-image, but only if you truly want it, plan for it, and work at it. No matter what methods you use, you may find these suggestions helpful:

- **Live in the present.** We can learn from past mistakes and even failures, but not by dwelling on them. Again, we should plan for the future and set some goals, but we must live our lives day by day.
- **Learn new things.** We need new information to meet new challenges. But information is not enough. We also must provide ourselves new experiences by finding creative ways to act on the new information.
- **Avoid discouragement.** We all make mistakes and often repeat them. This can be very discouraging and can tempt us to give up. Here is where we must be patient with ourselves and a little less judgmental. To repeat: Developing new habits is not easy, and changing our self-image is even more difficult, but both are well worth the effort.

For this program, these definitions are offered for the exercises in this session:

- **Self-image:** How you see yourself.
- **Self-esteem:** How you feel about yourself.
- **Self-affirmation:** What you do about improving the way you see and feel about yourself.

### Exercise One
*Write your responses in your notebook.*

1. At the time of your divorce how did you feel about yourself?
2. How did your self-esteem suffer because of your divorce?
3. List five to ten things that make you feel good about yourself today (for example, your looks, your competence, your integrity, being a good parent, being a good friend, etc.)

### Exercise Two
*Write your responses in your notebook. (These questions are based on material from* Design for Wholeness *by Sofield, Juliano and Hammett.)*

1. How would you rate your self-esteem on a scale of one to ten, with one being the lowest and ten being the highest?
2. What criteria did you use to make that judgment?

3. When has your self-esteem been the highest? What contributed to how high it was? How do you behave when your self-esteem is high?
4. In what one or two areas would you like to improve your self-image during this program?
5. Give examples of how the level of your self-image affects the way others react to you, either positively or negatively.

***Before the Next Session***
Read over the story of your marriage that you began in your notebook last week. Add to each chapter how you felt about yourself (self-esteem) and what you thought about your abilities and talents (self-image). Concentrate especially on your self-esteem then and your self-esteem now.

---

### For Stress
Take a few minutes *every day* to do something *just for you.* Don't allow others to intrude or make demands on that time. If you have a busy schedule, it might take some planning to ensure that this time is really your *free* time. Read a book, listen to music, relax with a cup of coffee or tea, take a leisurely bath or shower—anything that will make you feel good and give you a little space. This should be quiet, reflective time to help you gain some perspective on life.

---

## Self-Affirmation

It takes time, effort, determination and patience to make any real change in self-image. Logic and willpower, however, often need reinforcement, particularly in emotional times. You might find it helpful to use an image to fight an image. Try this one by Virginia Satir from her book *Peoplemaking*:

*Imagine yourself as a large pot. You control what goes into your pot, and what is taken out. Whatever is in your pot is what you must live with and is what you share with others. If your pot is full of negative feelings, only you can get rid of them. Similarly, if someone tries to dump more in, you can refuse to accept them. Better yet, if you decide to keep filling your pot with positive feelings, there won't be any space left for negative ones. Only you can decide what goes into your pot. You can do whatever is necessary to keep your pot filled with positive concepts that make you feel good about your life.*

Start putting something positive into your pot this week. Pick three or four of the following statements that appeal most to you. Repeat them to yourself five or six times a day for the next week. It often helps to give yourself reminders (write the statements on Post-its and stick them to the bathroom mirror, your bedside table, the refrigerator, the steering wheel of your car, etc.) This exercise may sound simplistic, but—as any person who has followed this program can tell you—you will come to believe in it. When you believe in it, you will act on it by incorporating these images into your self-affirmation efforts.

| | |
|---|---|
| I am OK | I am a caring person |
| I like me | I am special |
| I am interesting | I am understanding |
| I am a gentle person | I am loved |

# Session Three
# Stress

## Reflection One

The causes of stress aren't the same for everyone. What makes one person's heart pound might not faze someone else at all. Almost everyone, however, regards divorce as one of the most stressful things a person can go through. Researchers often rank it second only to a death in the family on lists of stressful life events. Unless it is dealt with constructively, the stress from divorce and the major life changes it involves can cause serious physical illness.

To be sure, stress is not always bad. We willingly put ourselves under stress when we compete, try to surpass a previous best, or strive to achieve a goal. Such forms of stress provide a natural high that gives a zest to living. Even so, living constantly in the fast lane takes a great deal of energy. Thinking we must live intensely all the time can put us under so much pressure that it can turn positive experiences into negative ones.

Anxiety is one of the primary contributors to stress. Anxiety is rooted in the fear of being hurt or suffering a loss, and it intensifies as we brace ourselves to face an impending danger. From experience, we learn to anticipate danger to ourselves and our families and try to take preventive action. For many of us, however, anxiety is caused not by imminent dangers but by remote or even imaginary ones. Most of the time, when we feel edgy, jittery, or nervous, it's because of unfounded worries and fear of the unknown. (Anxiety is often called the price one pays for having an active imagination.)

To apply this concept of anxiety to us divorced people, note the losses and fears caused by the major life changes we've undergone:

- **The loss of a loved one and a secure life.** Independence brings new risks and challenges, which are primary sources of fears.
- **The loss of even more control.** We often feel as if we have only slightly more control over our personal lives than we have over global problems. Our own emotions and everyday situations are

21

harder to handle. Other people seem to react differently to us than they did before our divorce. The feeling of being out of control creates the fear that no matter what we do, no matter how hard we try, things will still go wrong.

- **The loss of self-esteem.** We may worry more about appearing worthless to others or being ridiculed or embarrassed than we do about coping with our actual problems. (Such anxiety is not solely divorce-related. According to researchers, poor self-esteem causes more than 85 percent of all anxiety.)
- **The loss of identity.** Many divorced people fear having to relate to others in an entirely new way—as a single person—and having to adjust to unfamiliar ways of feeling, thinking and acting.

Another contributor to the stress of newly divorced people is the phenomenon known as the "flooding of emotions." This frightening experience often causes us to feel as if we are going crazy. Our emotions swing dramatically for no apparent reason. One minute we feel happy and ready to take on the world; the next we are depressed and unable to cope with even the simplest things. Our emotions are very close to the surface and easily triggered. Finding ourselves prone to accidents and given to nervous laughter and quick tears, we generally feel out of control. If we try to bottle up these feelings we become frustrated. If we dump our emotions on others, we feel embarrassed or guilty. This emotional see-sawing consumes a great deal of our energy—energy we need to work on our fundamental difficulties.

Fortunately, most of us not only survive such emotional crises, we also bounce back. We recognize that our worries and stresses can be signs of life and growth. We learn to accept the things that cannot be changed, develop the courage to change the things that can be changed, and find the wisdom to know the difference. This strategy keeps our stress to a manageable level.

### Exercise One
*Write your responses in your notebook.*

1. What were some of your biggest worries or fears at the time of your divorce?
2. What things are you most worried or anxious about now? How have things changed since your divorce?
3. Give one or two examples of how the "flooding of emotions" after your divorce caused problems for you. How have you learned to cope?

# Reflection Two

Being overloaded with too many things to do in too little time is another cause of stress. No matter how emotionally pressured we are, divorced people must deal with the hassles of everyday living. We still have jobs to do, bills to pay, children to care for, and other people's emotions (ideas, prejudices, preferences, interference, etc.) to deal with. Many of us feel the added pressure of being forced for the first time to assume full responsibility for major areas of our lives. To make matters worse, when we are overloaded we find it difficult to think objectively and manage as competently as we did before. The things we used to do on schedule are now done haphazardly, if at all. Everything in the day seems to run together. We feel irritable, frustrated and often depressed. Sometimes we become virtually immobilized. Other times we are able to take the major challenges in stride but are set off by petty annoyances, much to the confusion of our family and friends.

Up to this point we have concentrated on what causes stress in most people. But as we noted before, not everyone reacts the same way to the same situations. Differences in experiences are one important reason for the differences in reactions. A person who suffered poverty as a child might react strongly to even the suggestion of a lay-off. A person who was rejected or abandoned as a child probably would feel the trauma of a divorce more deeply than one who enjoyed a secure childhood. Understanding how experience affects your present feelings puts things into some perspective and can be an important tool in relieving anxiety and stress.

Although nothing can change people's history, other factors that affect their reactions to stressful situations can be changed. To list a few: how much rest and relaxation they get; how strong their faith is; how many close, supportive people they can rely on; how they care for their health; and how much pride they take in their accomplishments.

Divorcing people need to keep up their health to have enough energy to take control of their lives and build for the future. If stress can cause physical illness, all the way from headaches to heart attacks, it would seem prudent for divorcing people to take a long, hard look at the stress in their lives, assess its power to cause problems, and take steps to keep it at a manageable level.

*Exercise Two*
*Write your responses in your notebook.*

1. Think of one or two recent situations (positive or negative) that

23

were particularly stressful. Do you think this stress has affected your health? How?

2. How do you usually deal with stress? Does your strategy usually work? Why or why not?

### Before the Next Session

Whenever there is a serious change, good or bad, in any area of our lives, there are repercussions in other areas. A divorce is a very serious change, and it may well affect our relationship with God and our fellow church members. This week, add to your story of your marriage an account of how the events you recorded have affected your religious beliefs and practices. Even more importantly, try to identify the questions about God, faith, religion and even the Church that your divorce process has raised for you. Finally, recall the feelings you have experienced about God and religion during this time.

---

### Self-Affirmation

Continue trying to fight negative images of yourself with positive ones. Here is another starting place:

*Imagine your mind is a garden. The seeds, or images, you plant every day come from your beliefs about life. If you believe life to be dynamic, moving and growing, these are the images that will be planted in your subconscious. If you allow yourself to view life as boring, threatening, or even "over," these views will be absorbed into your subconscious. You can reap only what has been sown. If you continue to plant seeds of self-doubt, rejection or fear, you can expect to reap the weeds of more turmoil. If you turn the pattern around and begin sowing more positive images of yourself, you'll eventually be watching your crops grow, and you'll be gathering in the fruits of hope, peace and joy.*

Studies of the subconscious have shown that thoughts and ideas we have on our mind just before sleep seem to have a greater impact on the next day. Try "planting" one or two of these images in your imagination. It beats counting sheep!

| | |
|---|---|
| I have strengths | I will grow |
| I will learn | My problems can be solved |
| I will manage my life | Life is worth living |
| I will make decisions | The Lord helps those who help themselves |

---

24

## For Stress

For people under pressure, even an ordinary workload seems unbearable. Remind yourself that anxiety and tension are temporary states, and that you can work your way through your tasks. Try to eliminate as much as possible the feeling of being overloaded. Here are a few suggestions. Most of them deal with your attitudes or suggest activities for the times when you think your stress and anxiety are getting the better of you. Remember that success in managing stress will not come overnight, and it will not come at all if approached halfheartedly. It will take determination, persistence and time, but the results will be well worth the effort:

- **Work it out.** Do something physical to release pent-up energy. Take a walk, scrub a floor, do some gardening, go to the health club or gym, go for a bike ride, etc. You'll be able to handle your problems better when you're calm.
- **Give in occasionally.** If you find yourself in frequent confrontations, consider that *you* may be wrong. It's easier to give in once in a while, particularly when the issue isn't vital, rather than fight to prove you're right all the time. And when you yield a bit, others also are more willing to compromise, enabling you to work out your problems maturely.
- **Go easy with criticism.** Don't expect other people to follow your preconceived program—they have their own agendas. When you expect too much from others, you'll only feel frustrated and disappointed if they don't measure up. Try instead to search out their good points, and allow them the freedom to be themselves.
- **Give others a break.** When we are tense or anxious, we tend to become more competitive. Competitiveness is contagious, but so is cooperation. When you give others a break, you often make things easier for yourself. If others no longer feel threatened by you, they will stop being a threat to you.
- **Make yourself available.** Many newly divorced people think they are being left out, slighted or rejected, when in reality others are just waiting for them to make the first move. Give your friends, even those who were close to you and your ex-spouse when you were a couple, a chance to keep the friendship going. Strive to maintain a middle ground between withdrawing from social contacts and pushing yourself forward on every occasion.
- **Laugh a little—even at yourself.** A sense of humor works wonders in many high-pressure situations.
- **Do something for others.** If you are focusing too much on yourself, try doing something for someone else. This will ease some of your self-centered anxiety. Even better, it will give you some real satisfaction.

# Life Change Index Scale

Check the space on the right if the event has happened to you *in the last 12 months.* Follow the directions on page 28 to assess your probability of becoming ill because of stress.

1. Death of spouse ___ 100
2. Divorce finalized ___ 73
3. Marital separation begun ___ 65
4. Detention in jail or other institution ___ 63
5. Death of a close family member ___ 63
6. Major personal injury or illness ___ 53
7. New marriage ___ 50
8. Being fired ___ 47
9. Marital reconciliation ___ 45
10. Retirement ___ 45
11. Major change in the health or behavior
of a family member ___ 44
12. Pregnancy ___ 40
13. Sexual difficulties ___ 39
14. Gaining a new family member
*(birth, adoption, elder moving in, etc.)* ___ 39
15. Major business readjustment
*(merger, reorganization, bankruptcy, etc.)* ___ 38
16. Major change in financial state
*(a lot worse off or a lot better off)* ___ 37
17. Death of a close friend ___ 36
18. Changing to a different line of work ___ 36
19. Major change in the number of arguments
with spouse *(regarding child-rearing,
personal habits, etc.)* ___ 35
20. Taking on a mortgage greater than $100,000
*(buying a home, business, etc.)* ___ 31
21. Being foreclosed on a mortgage or loan ___ 30
22. Major change in responsibilities at work
*(promotion, demotion, lateral transfer)* ___ 29
23. Son or daughter leaving home
*(marriage, attending college, etc.)* ___ 29
24. In-law troubles ___ 29
25. Outstanding personal achievement ___ 28
26. Spouse beginning or ceasing work outside the home ___ 26

27. Beginning or ending formal schooling       __ 26
28. Major change in living conditions *(building or remodeling a home, deterioration of neighborhood)*       __ 25
29. Revision of personal habits *(dress, manners, associations, etc.)*       __ 24
30. Trouble with your boss       __ 23
31. Major change in working hours or conditions       __ 20
32. Change in residence       __ 20
33. Changing to a new school       __ 20
34. Major change in usual type and/or amount of recreation       __ 19
35. Major change in church activities *(a lot more or a lot fewer than usual)*       __ 19
36. Major change in social activities *(clubs, dancing, movies, visiting, etc.)*       __ 18
37. Taking on a debt or loan under $25,000 *(buying a car, boat, etc.)*       __ 17
38. Major change in sleeping habits *(a lot more or a lot less sleep or changes in sleep times)*       __ 16
39. Major change in number of family get-togethers *(a lot more or a lot fewer than usual)*       __ 15
40. Major change in eating habits *(changes in amount, hours, diet or surroundings)*       __ 15
41. Taking a vacation away from home       __ 13
42. Celebrating holidays with extended family       __ 12
43. Minor violations of the law *(traffic tickets, jaywalking, disturbing the peace, etc.)*       __ 11

*Adapted from "The Holmes and Rahe Social Readjustment Rating Scale"*

**Scoring the Scale**
Add up the number of points next to each of your check marks. Put the total on this line:

**TOTAL LIFE CHANGE UNITS (LCU)** _____

# Interpreting Your Score

Here are the score categories and the associated probability of illness during the next two years for a person with that score:

0-150—No significant increased chance of illness.
150-199—Mild Life-Crisis Level with a 35 percent chance
   of illness.
200-299—Moderate Life-Crisis Level with a 50 percent chance
   of illness.
300 or higher—Major Life Crisis Level with an 80 percent chance
   of illness.

Your score shows your *probability* of becoming ill through the stress in your life. The key factor on whether you in fact become ill, however, is how you deal with that stress.

# *Session Four*
# Anger

## Reflection One

Anger is a major emotion for most divorced people. We usually feel a great deal of it, have good reasons for it, and find plenty of people with whom to be angry. Sometimes the divorce itself is the cause of our anger. Other times it was there long before the separation, constantly simmering under the surface. Because anger affects so many relationships, two sessions in this program are devoted to examining it, talking it out, and accepting it for what it is.

In this session we'll explore what anger is and where it comes from. The first exercise will help you identify the people you're angry with, and why you are angry with them.

According to the dictionary, anger is "a feeling of extreme displeasure, hostility, indignation or exasperation toward someone or something." Like love, it is rarely logical or objective. If you ask people why they are angry, their answers will run the gamut from the sublime to the ridiculous, but the main theme is always a feeling of being wronged, threatened or frustrated.

Anger can be a good, positive emotion. When it is expressed appropriately, it can make people feel good about themselves, help relieve stress and tension, and make relationships with others more open and real. But most of us seldom associate our anger with feeling good. Although we may feel great letting off steam now and then, that's usually outweighed by remorse over what our anger does to others. No matter how justifiable our anger is, we usually end up feeling guilty about giving in to a "bad" emotion.

For divorced people, particularly those in early stages of the process, how we handle relationships is vital. It is therefore necessary for us to understand our anger, accept it, and learn to express it appropriately.

***Exercise One***
*Write your answers in your notebook.*

1. What made you the most angry when you realized your marriage was breaking up?
2. How did you handle your anger?
3. Who are you angry with now? List each person or group (e.g., ex-spouse, former in-laws, yourself, friends, God, church, co-workers, children, the "other woman" or "other man"). Briefly tell why you feel angry with each person or group and how your anger affects your daily life.

# Reflection Two

Understanding how our patterns of anger have developed can give us better insight into why we react the way we do now. Knowing this, we can find more constructive ways of dealing with anger—a powerful, complex emotion that has far-reaching effects on our lives.

We all first learned about anger from the families in which we grew up. That's where we saw what anger does to us and others and developed our feelings about it. Our first experience of anger probably was being pushed from our mother's womb into a cold, alien world. Coming from an atmosphere of total warmth, we found that our needs for food, shelter and love were not always met when and how we wanted. Mother didn't always jump to attention on cue; brothers and sisters offered competition; we were confronted with rules and regulations; and we were expected to do some things for ourselves.

By the time we were ready for school the real world had seriously intruded, creating more frustration. We learned to deal with our anger by observing those around us, particularly our parents. We saw how they expressed their anger toward us, toward each other, and toward outsiders. Within the family we learned acceptable ways of expressing anger that produced effects without costing too much love and approval.

Whatever patterns we adopted for expressing anger were further refined by our experiences as adults and reinforced by habit. If we were taught, for example, that anger was bad or that crying was only for babies or that you couldn't get mad at those you love, we became adept at denying, suppressing or disguising our anger.

All of this "training" in anger management can cause us serious problems with honest relationships as adults. In the next session we'll discuss some common patterns we follow in expressing our anger— some roles we play in dealing with others. Here we'll discuss our angry feelings, some ways we've learned to handle anger, and the effect it has on our lives today.

### Exercise Two
*Write your answers in your notebook.*

1. Think back to the ways your parents or other important people in your childhood handled anger. Describe ways in which their patterns influenced the way you deal with anger now.
2. How do you feel about the way you handle your anger? What changes do you wish you could make?

### Before the Next Session

Because anger is one of the strongest emotions divorced people have at this time, we want to make sure maximum time is allowed for discussing it. Therefore, we ask you sometime before Session Five to read the introductory material for it on pages 35-40 and give some concentrated thought to identifying some of the roles you might be assuming, perhaps without realizing it. In your journal make a note of any of these roles you frequently play.

Continue with your story in your journal. For each chapter or period of your life, write down the people with whom you were angry, how angry you were, and how you dealt with your anger. Especially concentrate on the anger you feel now as a result of your divorce. Transfer what you have written in the exercises in this session into your story, and expand on it if you can.

## Self-Affirmation

Here's a way to get another perspective on your self-image. In your journal draw a tree with deep, strong roots and rich foliage. Follow these instructions to complete the tree:

1. The roots of your tree are things you like about yourself. Fill in as many roots as you can. If you are unable to come up with 20 positive statements at one time, come back to it and add more later.
2. The leaves of your tree are all the positive things you hear others say about you. Listen for compliments and accept them gracefully. Enter them as you hear them daily.


## For Stress

Work on the structure of your daily life. How balanced are your eating, sleeping and exercise patterns? Keep a diary this week of what, when and how much you do in all three of these important areas. Be honest. Don't hide, excuse or gloss over your excesses or failures. Working out a true balance in your everyday life is too important to your overall health.

# On Prayer

Prayer is extremely helpful in times of stress, although the pain from your divorce may have tempted you to pray less often or with less enthusiasm. Here are three approaches to consider when you feel the need to pray:

A simple response to God. As you go through the day, tell God what's on your mind—that you are glad or angry, happy or hurt, or that you need help. Just take a minute or so; speak to God as you speak to a friend. Just speak your mind.

Centering prayer. This special type of prayer allows God's love to permeate your being. It is a restful state that comes from emptying the mind of distracting thoughts. Follow this pattern: Become comfortable in a quiet place and close your eyes. Concentrate on a phrase you like (e.g., "Jesus," "Lord," "Love," "Jesus loves me.") Combine this with some breathing exercises. Repeat the phrase you have chosen in rhythm, inhaling on one syllable or part of a phrase and exhaling on the rest. Repeat this breathing exercise five times slowly. When you are ready, sit in silence in the presence of God. Listen to God speaking within your solitude. Remain in this position as long as you wish. Slowly open your eyes and rest for a few minutes.

Meditation fantasy. A fantasy is an imaginative story in which you are one of the main characters. Using a scriptural passage as a setting for a fantasy gives you the opportunity to get in touch with God's love for you as well as to form your response to God. Read a passage in the Gospels describing an action Jesus performed. Imagine the setting of the action (the lake in Galilee, a grassy knoll under a tree, etc.) Close your eyes and place yourself at the scene as one of the characters. Allow the images to flow and extend the story. What do you see, touch, hear? What do you feel? What do you say to Jesus? How does he respond to you? What is Jesus doing while you're talking? What are you doing? Remain in the setting for a while. How does Jesus say goodbye when it's time to leave? How do you say goodbye? Remember that you can return to your fantasy anytime you wish.

# Session Five
# More on Anger

**Before We Begin**
Please read the Reflection prior to the session.

## Reflection

In her book *How to Get Angry without Feeling Guilty,* Adelaide Bry has described most of the masks people put on when they're angry. She has called these behavior patterns "roles." Here is a summary of these roles, together with suggestions on dealing with problems that can arise from playing each of them. As you read about these roles, see if you can identify some of your own patterns.

### The Actor

Actors create scenes, dramatizing their anger. They slam doors, pound tables, break dishes, brandish fists, and use other forms of dramatic body language. They are often described as quick-tempered or hotheaded.

Actors are not always deeply angry. In fact, they may be far less angry than an inwardly seething person. They are simply very quick to display and dramatize their feelings.

**Suggestion**: Making a scene may give you temporary relief, because it lets you get anger out of your system, but the person at whom you directed the anger may continue to stew. Too much venting of anger can strain your relationships with your family and friends. Look at yourself through the eyes of the person with whom you are interacting. How does the Actor's dramatic demonstration affect you?

### The Big Talker

Talking things out can clear the air, get our feelings across, and help us understand each other better. There are good and bad ways of talking, but Big Talkers, in order to alleviate their anger, insist that other

35

people listen to them a great majority of the time. They work very hard at learning to express themselves, but they aren't very good at listening in return. Here are five common types of Big Talkers:

- **Basic Big Talkers** get immediate physical and emotional release from quick verbal explosions or long verbal rants.
- **Leakers** verbalize their anger, but only in dribs and drabs and often with a smile.
- **Truth-Tellers** feel free to say anything, as long as it's true.
- **Commentators** are convinced that any attempt to suppress their anger is bad for them, so they comment angrily on everyone and everything.
- **Verbal Self-Haters** enjoy telling how they have messed up their marriage, their children, their career, their whole life.

**Suggestion**: If you are a Big Talker, practice listening. Listen to what you say, to the way you say it, and to what others say.

## The Blamer

Blamers don't take responsibility for the way they act or feel toward others, nor do they hold themselves accountable for their actions. They often say things such as "She's driving me crazy" or "He'll be sorry." They use anger as a device to protect themselves, holding onto it until they find a target on which to blame their unhappiness. By blaming others for everything, they "prove" that they are fine.

**Suggestion**: Ask yourself why you are blaming others. Are they really 100 percent wrong, and are you really 100 percent right? No one can make us feel a particular emotion. In most cases we choose how we view something that someone else does and react in different ways (with anger, pity, amusement, etc.) as a result. If you honestly and calmly conclude that someone is wronging you, take up the matter directly with that person (even if it's your former spouse). Even then, don't express blame. Simply describe your feelings and the situation in matter-of-fact terms, using "I" expressions, such as "I felt angry when you..." or "I felt hurt when you...."

## The Body Person

Body People desperately want to project a good, sweet, kind, lovable image. To express anger is to admit to themselves and others that they aren't perfect. So they suppress their anger, which causes physical ailments—colds, high blood pressure, etc. Although the causes are psychological, the problems are real and call for consulting a doctor.

**Suggestion**: Confront your anger, look at it, feel it, and accept it as part of yourself. Understand that having angry feelings does not make you evil. When you're able to focus on the source of your anger, have an imaginary conversation with the people involved and really "let them have it." You'll feel better.

## The Comedian

If you can make others laugh and have a reputation as quick-witted and clever, you probably also use humor to express and deal with your anger. Natural-born comedians, having effortless wit and minds and tongues that work as one, can produce a steady stream of satirical anecdotes, wisecracks and jokes. They can goad with gentle irony or launch a slashing verbal attack that leaves the victim gasping in disbelief. And all the while the comedians pretend it's all in fun.

**Suggestion**: Don't stop the funny business. We need all the laughter we can get. But be careful not to use humor as a weapon. Ask yourself how much of it is hurtful. Watch the facial expressions of those at whom your humor is directed. Think back to the last time you were angry and knew it, and expressed your anger with hostile humor. How do you think the person you targeted felt?

## The Cornered Person

Cornered People learned as children that showing and expressing anger meant getting sent to bed, to another room, or to a corner. The degree of their secretiveness, depression or self-hatred corresponds to how much and in what ways they were physically or emotionally punished in the past for being angry. A couple of variations:

• **Drowners** try to dull their anger with alcohol or drugs.
• **Self-Destroyers** take their enormous bag of emotion and allow it to bury them, sometimes literally.

**Suggestion**: Try writing: "I am angry at...."; "I am angry at...because...."; "I am angry at...because...and I want to...." Fill in the blanks with whoever or whatever comes into your mind first. Go into detail—no entries that say "I'm angry with myself because I'm a lazy bum." Write "I'm mad at myself because I forgot Tom's birthday." Then ask yourself whether you are really angry with yourself or whether you're mad at Tom for something. Perhaps that's the real reason you "forgot" his birthday. In other words, try to determine whether you are truly angry with yourself or reacting to another person or set of circumstances.

## The Scene Creator

Scene Creators simply can't leave well enough alone. They need to stir things up. They claim they enjoy a good argument to relieve monotony, but what they're really after is an opportunity to let off steam. Scene Creators tend to pick out a scapegoat, make that person the butt of their anger, and frequently lash out at him or her. Scene Creators have an especially large bag of "free-floating" anger. They create scenes for a reason—to get relief from the tension they feel constantly. They also use their anger to assume a power position in a group.

**Suggestion**: Reduce your persistent muscular tension by exercising. If you have scapegoats, make a conscious effort to stop unloading on them. Think back to the last time you were a Scene Creator: What were the costs and payoffs of playing this role? How might you express your anger in more productive ways?

## The Daydreamer

In fantasy, the timid turn bold, the weak grow strong, the clumsy become graceful, the tongue-tied discover eloquence. In the privacy of our minds, we can all rise up in righteous wrath and set things right. Most people are daydreamers at least part of the time, and that's fine. It's a relatively safe and harmless way to get rid of excess anger. The key question is: Does the fantasy relieve your anger so you can deal with the real-life problem more calmly, or at least enable you to turn to other matters?

A more dangerous variation of the Daydreamer is the **Escapist**. Escapists use fantasies not as a healthy release but to avoid reality. Escapism may help you get rid of pent-up anger, but it won't solve your problems.

**Suggestion**: The next time you find yourself slipping into a daydream, stop and come back to reality. Ask yourself why you're angry. Once you're clear about the problem that has caused your feelings, decide whether daydreaming is an appropriate way to handle it. If most of your daydreams revolve around your divorce, try to change the focus of those fantasies. Direct them toward discovering new ways to deal with your problems in the real world.

## The Doer

Doers are the opposite of Body People, who bring on physical ailments by keeping anger inside their bodies. Doers' bodies act as open-ended conductors: Instead of accumulating angry energy, they use it. "Doing" is healthy when you are aware of what's happening. However, there's a big difference between deliberately working on your anger, which is healthy, and burying it in activity, which may be a form of escapism. Some Doers develop ingenious ways of working anger out of their systems—jogging in place, weeding, working in the yard, scrubbing floors, aerobic dancing, walking.

**Suggestion**: Ask yourself what is causing your tension. Write down your responses. Once you understand what's bothering you, you'll be in a better position to decide whether to continue the things you are "doing."

### The Saboteur
Saboteurs express anger indirectly. They become chronic forgetters, losers, breakers, spillers, burners, latecomers. When they are confronted on their annoying habits, they feel victimized and misunderstood. At the same time, they get pleasure from being the center of attention. (Even the most careless Saboteurs manage to keep their wits about them when the stakes are high, which proves they really do have control over themselves.)

Saboteurs also exercise control over others, albeit in indirect ways. They make others suffer, but they do it without experiencing the discomfort of being held responsible for their actions. They may appear to be vague or befuddled in certain circumstances, thus escaping unpleasant duties and frustrating others. They tend to interrupt people who are speaking. Another favorite tactic is covering their hostility with expressions of boredom.

**Suggestion**: Think back to the last time you were a Saboteur. How did you control or manipulate the situation? Who was your victim and how did that person react? Now imagine yourself on the receiving end of that sabotage. Go back through the experience and think of more constructive ways of handling the control issues.

### The Stuffer
Stuffers assume that if they don't get angry at you, you won't get angry at them. They mask their feelings with an attitude of "Grin and bear it" or "What do I care?" They learned as children that feelings are not important and that expressing them can lead to trouble. Some people have stuffed their feelings for so long that they have a chronic sense of unease and disquiet. They feel something is wrong, but they are unable to identify it as anger. Other stuffers are aware of their anger but are too scared to do anything about it. They fear either retaliation from others or that they'll lose control of themselves. They

may even be wary of intellectual stimulation, lest it lead to conflict, which might make them angry and risk their standing as gentle, controlled people. Overeating is another common expression of this role.

**Suggestion:** Try to imagine the worst thing that could happen to you if you verbalized your anger, and then find a way to express the anger in a safe setting (alone or with a close friend or counselor, for example). After you have practiced, you might decide stuffing is still the best policy in most cases, but in others you may decide to speak out. When you learn to say respectfully what's on your mind, you'll discover that others usually can handle your anger.

### Exercise One
*Write your answers in your notebook.*

1. Reflecting on these roles can bring us some insights into how we express, suppress and repress our angry feelings. Which roles best describe the way you express your anger?
2. In Session Four you listed some people at whom you are angry now. Select people from your list and answer these questions about each one:
   • Briefly describe the incident or situation you are angry about.
   • Which of the roles (you may chose more than one) did you play?
   • What was the result, and how do you feel about how you handled the situation?
3. Talk with your friends or your *Divorce and Beyond* group about how you might express your anger more constructively.

### Exercise Two
*Write your answers in your notebook.*

When you become angry with someone, chances are that person will become angry with you, and you will both begin to play different roles. You can't control the way others act, but you can control your own actions and be aware of the patterns that others use. Then you can respond in ways that can be helpful to both of you.

1. Draw a three-column table like this in your notebook:

| Person | Name | Role others played | Role you played |
|--------|------|--------------------|-----------------|
| 1 | | | |
| 2 | | | |
| 3 | | | |

- Write the names of two or three people you deal with who are important to you (including your former spouse if you are still in contact).
- List the anger roles these people play.
- List the roles you usually play when you become angry with these people.
- Try to describe what usually happens with each person. For example: "My former spouse is a Stuffer. I am an Actor. When I get mad, I say what I think. My former spouse considers this 'blowing up again,' feels bad, but won't fight back. I wind up apologizing but I'm still mad. Few things get discussed this way, much less resolved."
- Try using a new strategy with each person on your list and see what happens when you stop playing your usual role or roles. Does the other person also change the way he or she acts?

2. Discuss with a friend or your *Divorce and Beyond* group one or more of the situations you listed.
3. If you have not read the suggestions after each of the roles described above, do so now.

***Before the Next Session***
The way we handle anger often changes over time. Look at your marriage "story" and write about how you've handled anger at different times. Note especially two or three very important times when you changed the way you expressed anger. Reflect on and write why you think you are handling your anger the way you do now. If you think you could use help handling your anger more constructively, practice one of the suggestions in the reading.

By understanding how your early training and present circumstances have influenced how you handle anger, you can stop being so hard on yourself for recent shortcomings. Better yet, you may find that not everything you've done is wrong, and you may learn how to deal with those things that are wrong. If this process doesn't help after a period of time, you may want to seek professional help.

---

### Self-Affirmation

Pretend you are your own best friend. During the week write a short profile of yourself from your friend's viewpoint. Try developing the profile by adding a little to it each day.

### For Stress

Recreation is essential for your physical and mental health. Take time for doing the things you enjoy. This week, find an activity or hobby you can throw yourself into and forget your problems for a while.

# Some Hints On Changing Behavior

If we want to change a behavior, it is not enough to say "I will not act like that anymore." We must choose a different way of acting with definite steps to follow:

Step 1. Clearly identify the behavior you want to change.
Step 2. Get in touch with your feelings about that behavior.
Step 3. Decide on a new way of behaving.
Step 4. Start practicing it for a week in specific but workable ways. Don't try anything so difficult that you set yourself up for failure.
Step 5. Evaluate this new way of acting. If it works, keep practicing it until it becomes a habit.

# *Session Six*
# Blame and Guilt

## Reflection One

Rarely is it fair for one person in a newly divorced couple to take all the blame or feel all the guilt. In this session we'll explore both blame and guilt and try to gain some perspective on who's at fault. You? Your former spouse? Others? No one?

In Session One you began writing down your account of your marriage and divorce, changing it as your perspective on the "story" changed. Many of us who follow this suggestion start to tell our stories by assigning blame for the failure of the relationship—to ourselves, our former spouses, and a host of others. The need to blame somebody or something is almost standard operating procedure in the aftermath of most divorces, even when both spouses agreed that divorce was the only realistic solution in their situation.

Some of us are chronic blamers who never assume responsibility for our actions. We blame someone else or shrug off our own behavior with a "devil made me do it" attitude. It's almost as if our survival depends on being right and holding power.

Others of us are masters at blaming ourselves for everything. We assign ourselves full responsibility for everything that has gone wrong. We "ruined" our wonderful marriage by being too clever, too dull, too critical, too careless, having (or not having) children, etc. Such self-blame can assume almost supernatural overtones when we believe that we alone control every situation.

Still others of us try to assign blame for our divorce among many people, including family, friends, colleagues, our former partners, and ourselves. Though this approach appears a little more even-handed, we have the same problem as all other blamers: We feel justified in exacting guilt from those we blame.

But what if you honestly think you have been wronged or injured? How can you express your anger without falling into and staying in the blaming trap? You have already taken the first step: You have begun to look at yourself and others honestly and have put your divorce into some sort of perspective. The exercises in this session should give you a few more insights.

### *Exercise One*
*Write your responses in your notebook.*

1. If you were to divide the responsibility for the breakup of your marriage among several people and situations, what percentage of the blame would you assign to the people and things listed here? Don't strive for statistical accuracy, but it would help if the figures added up to 100%.

| | | | |
|---|---|---|---|
| Yourself | ___% | Your job | ___% |
| Your former spouse | ___% | Your former spouse's job | ___% |
| Your extended family | ___% | Money | ___% |
| Your in-laws | ___% | Sex | ___% |
| Your children | ___% | Religion | ___% |
| The "other" man or woman | ___% | Other | ___% |

2. List in your notebook the two or three people or situations you blame the most. (Do not include yourself here. We will deal with self-blame and guilt in Exercise Two.) Jot down some of your reasons for holding these people or situations responsible.
3. How has your relationship with these people been affected by the way you feel toward them?

## Reflection Two

All human beings are imperfect. We are all fallible and often fall short of the standards we set for ourselves. When we do, it is normal and healthy to feel guilty. However, when two or more people are involved (and particularly in a divorce), it is unreasonable to assume that one person should feel all the guilt. It is also unreasonable for anyone to feel guilty all the time.

Many of us also carry around bags of guilty feelings when we are not really guilty at all. Here are some occasions that typically make some people feel imposed or unrealistic guilt:

- Doing something that goes against a social norm but is not necessarily a moral issue.

- Doing something that goes against the values, rules or regulations of other people.
- Doing something with the best of intentions that turns out badly.
- Assuming responsibility for a situation over which we have little or no control.

When we have carried around bags of guilt for years, it takes time and concentration to sort out our feelings and learn to accept only the guilt that we conclude we really should. Here again, daily efforts to grow deeper in self-knowledge and self-acceptance will be invaluable. Only by knowing and valuing ourselves as God values us can we accept our humanity and judge ourselves honestly and gently. Real guilt occurs only when we freely choose to do something that goes against our own deeply held moral values. ((Those who feel guilty or bad all the time might need professional help to gain a more balanced perspective.)

We cannot rely on others to tell us what to do in every situation. We are expected to have a deeply ingrained set of values that we can honestly say is real for us. These values make up the cornerstone of an informed conscience that can help us make adult choices and accept responsibility for the results.

A conscience that is a wise guide rather than a stern taskmaster is rooted in self-knowledge. It accepts that human beings are capable of both good and evil. It recognizes that we must forgive ourselves for our flaws and mistakes. Finally, it allows us to respect ourselves enough to allow a little space for living and making choices. With such a conscience comes the understanding that sin can proceed only from inside each individual. Others cannot impose sin, so others should not impose guilt.

The Church can help those of us who want to address our wrongdoing and feelings of guilt. Catholics can receive forgiveness from sin through the Sacrament of Reconciliation. In confession we must face ourselves and acknowledge our guilt, verbalize it, and externalize it so we can free ourselves from its grip. The absolution a priest gives us follows the absolution we must first give ourselves. (Ministers of other denominations and religions also can help us acknowledge sin, even if the forgiveness doesn't come in the form of a sacrament. They can help us believe that God forgives us and understand how important it is for us to forgive ourselves.)

When we become more fully aware of who we are, we can reach a state where we are no longer controlled by inner compulsions or others' expectations. We can look instead to that "inner court," where our own conscience becomes the plaintiff, judge and jury. When we

47

render a verdict of "guilty" on ourselves, we can then ask for forgiveness from a loving God, who understands we are human. We can also ask forgiveness from those we've injured and do whatever is necessary to make amends. Finally, we can stop punishing ourselves and take charge of our lives.

### Exercise Two
*Write your responses in your notebook.*

---

**Note:** *These questions are very personal. Share with the group or your friends only to the degree that you are comfortable.*

---

1. Imagine someone saying these things to you. Jot down the first reaction that comes to your mind.
   - "It's your fault that...."
   - "If only you had...."
   - "I couldn't help it! You made me...."
   - "Without you to hold me back, I would have...."

2. What is making you feel guilty as a result of your divorce?
3. Which of these guilty feelings do you think grew out of imposed or unrealistic guilt? Which grew out of a sense of real guilt?
4. What were some of the ways you tried to deal with these guilty feelings?

### Before the Next Session
To make choices and act on your own values, you must once again look at your life "story" and remember as best you can two or three values that were most important to you at different times in your life. The most important time in that "story" is the present. Try to be as clear as you can about which values you think guide you today. It may help to put them into two groups: Values that carry moral connotations (e.g., the Ten Commandments), and values that add richness and pleasure to your life (e.g., music and sports).

### Self-Affirmation

Do something special for yourself this week. Tell yourself you are doing it just because you deserve it. Reward yourself for all the good, positive things you've done since you began the *Divorce and Beyond* program.


### *For Stress*

Too often when we feel particularly stressed, a vacation seems to be the only thing that could help us. But we usually can't schedule a vacation on the spur of the moment. Taking a short "Two-Minute Vacation" through the use of guided imagery, however, can help you slow down and ease some tension. With practice, this exercise becomes easier and more beneficial. It can be done almost anywhere that you have a few minutes to spare.

**Instructions**: Sit in a comfortable chair in a quiet spot. Relax by slowing down your breathing. Slowly inhale through your nose and imagine you are breathing in from your toes, filling yourself up with air. As you slowly exhale through your mouth, let go of any tension you feel in your head, face, jaw, neck, shoulders, back, chest, abdomen, legs and feet. Repeat this breathing exercise three times. Now close your eyes and create a peaceful scene in your mind, and imagine yourself in that scene. Let whatever thoughts come to mind flow. After several minutes, open your eyes and enjoy the feeling.

# On Conscience and the Catholic Church

It is often hard for people to identify the values they can use to guide their choices. For Catholics, the teachings of the Church are a definite source of values. Nevertheless, many people have serious conscience problems when they try to apply the rules and regulations they learned in their youth to the complex issues they face as adults. Others, finding that the old answers do not always work now, feel betrayed and dismiss all the teachings. In doing so, they throw out the baby with the bathwater. Those who have not kept current with the many Church teachings since Vatican II may be unsure of the Catholic positions on the moral questions they have. Asking questions of knowledgeable people, studying Church teaching, and participating in an RCIA (Rite of Christian Initiation of Adults) program might provide some answers.

# Session Seven
# Loneliness

## Reflection One

*"It is not good for man to be alone."* In this one famous line, *Genesis* highlights one of the greatest needs for all human beings: relationships with others. We need to love and be loved. We need a safe, warm and supportive environment. We must know that we are important to others and that our lives and destinies are intermingled with theirs. Being cut off from close relationships brings on an array of feelings that are inadequately labeled "loneliness."

It seems natural for us to assume that when we marry, our partner will meet all our relational needs. Indeed, many people marry just to escape their fear of loneliness, but if their marriage fails to make them feel needed, loved and safe, they feel betrayed as well as lonely. This is usually the first sign that the "lingering death" of the relationship is under way. Simply sharing the same space with someone does not necessarily mean being emotionally close, much less being partners— or "two in one flesh," as *Genesis* puts it.

When we divorce, we see changes in the support systems we took for granted while we were married. Besides losing the physical and emotional support of our former partner, we often find that the dynamics have changed between us and many of our secondary supports. Even our relationships with our own extended families are rarely the same, to say nothing of our involvement with our former spouse's families. Holiday celebrations that once were a joy may turn into complicated, awkward affairs. Friends and neighbors often have difficulty adjusting to socializing with us as a single person. Very few of our comfortable, automatic associations remain the same after a divorce.

We react to these changes in ways as diverse as our personalities. However, some reactions are common for newly divorced people, especially in those of us who feel completely rejected or cut off. Our first response is to escape the pain by pulling back, like someone whose hand has been burned. We retreat from involvement with other people to avoid being hurt again. Or we devote all our time and energy to working, parenting or some other activity. We keep physically and mentally busy to fill the emotional vacuum. On the other hand, some of us who initially married to escape loneliness cling obsessively to others after our divorce to avoid the pain of being alone again.

All of these reactions to loneliness work to some extent, but only temporarily. Eventually, avoiding our problems becomes a self-defeating habit. (A special danger at this time is to fall into the habit of abusing alcohol or drugs in an effort to escape or at least dull the pain.)

Sooner or later, we must accept the changes in our support systems that come as a result of our marriages ending. We must begin to reinforce and strengthen relationships with those people and things that remain in our lives and seek out new relationships and activities.

The first step is to stay as close as possible to our family and friends. Relatives tend to take each other for granted, but when a crisis forces us to think about and readjust to each other, we often become closer than we were before. Church contacts and support groups are another safe way to deal with loneliness.

We divorced people inevitably seek out new friends. This is not easy for those of us who are not assertive or who have lived in a couple-centered world for a long time. After years of the married lifestyle, it is a challenge to start learning new things. However, being open to new people, ideas and experiences is one of the first steps to accepting our new life. Real friendships are formed when we allow ourselves the freedom to be who we really are and allow others that same freedom.

Reaching out requires us to take risks. Testing the waters and being open to new experiences is what everyone has to do to keep from feeling lonely. No one can avoid occasional times of feeling rootless and disconnected. But these periods will be far less frequent and intense for those of us who build and maintain close friendships and seek out new and rewarding experiences than they will for those who brood in fear and self-pity.

One word of caution: Until we are truly connected with our self-worth and have really worked through our "mourning period" after a divorce, we should be very wary of becoming seriously involved with another person. Rushing into a serious relationship too soon, just to fill a void, may only lead to our further disillusionment.

*Exercise One*
*Write your responses in your notebook.*

1. Reflect back on two or three times during the last few months when you felt particularly lonely. What did you do to break out of it? Did it help?
2. Name the people to whom you turn for help in coping with your loneliness.
3. What has been your experience in trying to make new friends since your marriage ended?
4. What image of yourself are you trying to project to these new friends?

# Reflection Two

Reflection One dealt with our need for external support systems to live happy and fulfilled lives. These are only part of what we need in our struggle with loneliness, however. Those of us who have inner resources will be better able to deal with our loss and the challenge of adjusting to new roles in our life.

Long after our separation and divorce, many of us are still haunted by a gnawing, unidentifiable feeling that something is missing. We think of ourselves as "people without"—as somehow incomplete.

It is natural to have a deep feeling of loss when we lose our spouse. Certainly, just having a warm body missing from the bed next to us contributes a great deal to this feeling. But it goes deeper. Some of us believe our emotional survival is actually dependent on another person.

One divorced woman said she went from being someone's daughter to being someone's wife to being someone's mother. She never identified herself as "just me." After her divorce she was forced to grow from being dependent on others to being independent of others—sure enough of her own identity to provide a sense of family for herself and her children. She had to look within herself for the resources to make it on her own. In taking an inventory of her strengths, knowledge, talents and personality, she found a unique, complete person whom she actually liked and respected. This woman still sorely misses all the good things she lost from her past life. Being without them still hurts. Nevertheless, she has learned to remember what she has lost without feeling that a part of herself is missing. She can reach out to others, not to "complete" herself but to make her life richer and fuller.

When we reach this point of acceptance of ourselves as complete and unique human beings, we can even appreciate the advantages of being alone every now and then. We can savor whatever time and space we can grab for ourselves to assimilate new perceptions and experiences. We welcome the freedom to shed any false postures we may have assumed to please our former mate and the chance to integrate into our personalities elements we may have hidden for years.

Those of us who are at peace with ourselves (and we are many) can accept our loneliness as an authentic part of life. Because we know we are as worthy of being loved as we are capable of loving others, we can reach out with confidence to new people and new experiences.

### *Exercise Two*
*Write your responses in your notebook.*

1. What positive images come to mind when you hear the word "alone"? Draw one or more of these images.
2. What negative images come to mind when you hear the word "lonely"? Draw one or more of them.
3. When you were married, what roles did you feel you had to play (as opposed to being yourself) with your spouse, children, friends and others?
4. Now that you are single, in what ways do you feel more complete as a person? In what ways do you feel less complete?

### *Before the Next Session*
Refer to your written "story" again. Read your entries for the stages in your life and try to remember the times during each stage that you felt particularly lonely. To the best of your recollection, write for each chapter why you felt so intensely isolated—as opposed to simply alone—on these occasions, and what you did about it.

The losses you've experienced because of your divorce most likely have intensified your overall feelings of loneliness. Take some quiet time and make a list of some of the small, perhaps insignificant things you miss from your married life (for example, not having to drive all the time, a balanced checkbook, the park across from your old house.) The emotions you will be dealing with here will be difficult enough without trying to start with the hard things. Try writing a letter—to yourself, to another person, or to the loss itself—to say goodbye to just one of the losses you've listed. You don't have to show the letter to anyone. Its purpose is to help you work through your emotions, to recognize that you can miss things and experiences as well as people, and to finally let go of them. (If you find yourself becoming too upset while you are writing the letter, put it aside for a while and finish it when you are more composed.)

### Self-Affirmation

Recognize your successes each day. Write them down in your notebook. Give special emphasis to the talents, strengths and qualities it took you to achieve what you did. Enjoy your successes. They are real. They are honest. They are yours!

### For Stress

Imagine putting all of your painful, depressing thoughts in a boat and pushing it out to sea. Watch it float away.

—OR—

Carry on an imaginary conversation with someone who causes you stress or anxiety. Start by saying what you've always wanted to tell this person but have been afraid to say face-to-face. Shift mental gears and respond as you think that person would. Keep the conversation going until you can design the ending you want. (If you have difficulty imagining yourself as the other person, place two chairs facing each other. Sit in one chair as you start your "conversation" and move to the other when you answer. Keep moving between the two chairs as you continue. This technique will help you assume the role of the other and verbalize what you think and feel.) This exercise will help you understand other people's point of view, and you may find yourself becoming less judgmental—of others as well as yourself.

# A Note on Time

One thing we never seem to have enough of is time. After looking at how we spend our time, we may be able to plan improvements. Break up the time you spend into three categories:

- **Diffused time.** This is time you spend doing the everyday activities that do not require your undivided attention. Sometimes you can even do several of them at the same time. This is probably by far how most of your day is spent. Because things get done during this time, the results are easy to measure.
- **Optimum time.** This is the very special time you spend with people who are of great value to you. You want to deal with these people on a personal, one-to-one basis and give them your undivided attention. This is the most important time you have. Yet in trying to keep pace with your busy schedule, you might shortchange yourself and those you care about, because we all tend to assume that those we love and who love us will always understand and that we will have time for them in the future. If you feel the need to improve here, you can start by reminding yourself that it takes time to develop and maintain those relationships. Remember also that time is a two-way street. Our "optimum time" people often have limitations on their time as well, so unless you work at making time for one other, you'll likely drift into taking your loved ones for granted.
- **Individual time.** This is the time you spend just on yourself. It is uninterrupted, quiet time to read, listen to music, daydream, pray—whatever relaxes you and contributes to your peace and happiness. Individual time will be the hardest for you to find right now. Some of us who feel lonely hesitate to *plan* time to be alone, even to do something we might enjoy. Others of us are tempted to go to the other extreme and withdraw from people as much as possible. We spend too much time living in the past and refusing to face new situations. Some individual time is obviously a necessity, but how much is a personal decision based on your own needs.

# *Session Eight*
# Forgiveness

## Reflection

Life is so filled with hard things, misplays, and misunderstandings of all kinds that it somehow does not seem quite fair that on top of these we are expected to forgive others for their faults. It can't be forgiveness just in words; it has to be real or it does not work at all. Forgiveness, according to the Scriptures, must come from the heart and that, of course, is exactly what makes it so hard. When we do something from our heart we are doing something with our whole person....

We cannot be forgiving, however, unless we can first admit that we can be vengeful and hard of heart. We do not even experience our own personality unless we take a close look at those parts of ourselves that we would ordinarily prefer to disown. We would rather push these feelings down or hide them in a haze of forgetfulness. But then we are only trying to bury a part of ourselves.... Forgiveness of ourselves, it is commonly said, is necessary before we can forgive anyone else. This begins by admitting just how complex and contradictory we can sometimes be in our personal relationships. Forgiveness starts when we can recognize the fullness of our faulted selves in the human condition and not turn away. Forgiveness is accomplished when we can take responsibility for all that we are....

There is a marvelous freedom that comes to us when we have the courage to see ourselves pretty much as we are. It is this freedom that gives us the power to forgive others. And that power, of course, is none other than the power of love itself, the love that comes in life when we are truly in touch with the persons we are. Only this love enables us to redeem others and ourselves through the kind of forgiveness that is tempered in the cleansing fires of self-examination and self-acceptance.

**From *The Pain of Being Human* by Eugene C. Kennedy**

Forgiveness is not a feeling; it is a decision. When we forgive those who have injured us, we acknowledge our respect for their rights and feelings as well as our own. This does not imply that we deny the hurt, and it doesn't necessarily mean we want close relationships with the people we forgive. It means we want to free ourselves of the burdens of grievances we have against people. In the final analysis, forgiveness is a gift we give ourselves.

Be aware that unconditional forgiveness often takes a long time to achieve. We first must make a decision to forgive, and then we must work step by step to achieve it. It may take us a long time, and we may never get there completely. But it is better to start than to remain mired in our resentments.

### Exercise One
*Write your responses in your notebook.*

1. List two or three people you are still blaming for hurting you. Begin by putting your name first on the list—true forgiveness must begin with forgiving yourself. Then write the other names.
2. Here are statements about forgiving people. Jot down next to each name on your list (including your own) the letter or letters of the statements that most closely describe how you feel about forgiving that person at this time.

a. I don't even want to think about forgiving this person.
b. I'll forgive this person because God will get him/her for me!
c. I'll forgive this person, but I can't forget (nor will I let him/her forget, either!)
d. I'll try to forgive this person, but only if I can avoid having much to do with him/her.
e. When I think about forgiving this person, I get mad all over again.
f. I can't forgive this person, because what he/she did to me was simply unforgivable.
g. I can't forgive this person, but I do not wish him/her any harm.
h. I want to forgive this person, but I just can't yet.
i. I'm finding it easier to forgive this person because I have a little more understanding of why he/she acted that way.
j. I'm finding it easier to forgive this person because I don't think he/she meant to hurt me that way.
k. I'm finding it easier to forgive this person now that I no longer

see myself through his/her eyes. It doesn't matter what he/she thinks or does.

l. I sometimes think I have forgiven this person, but then the anger returns. I go back and forth between anger and forgiveness.

m. I'm praying for the ability to forgive this person.

n. I forgive this person fully. Now that I'm no longer controlled by my anger, I feel free.

3. To start the process of forgiving, write one or two small things next to each name on your list for which you can forgive that person right now. (Don't forget to forgive yourself for something.)

4. What else can you do to start or continue the process of forgiving yourself?

### *Exercise Two*

This is a group exercise. If you are not part of a *Divorce and Beyond* group, you might try it with three or four close friends.

Sometimes those who anger or hurt us may not intend to do so at all. They may not even know they have caused us pain. In this exercise we will try to look at possible reasons why someone did something that hurt us and see if we can arrive at a better understanding of that person.

- On a file card or piece of paper, write a situation in which someone (not in the group) made you very angry. Describe it in as little or as much detail as you want. Do not put your name on the card.

- Put your card or sheet in the center of the table with the writing facing down. All the cards get mixed up and are put back in the center.

- Each person takes one card. If you get your own, return it and take another. Try to put yourself in the place of the person who *caused* the anger in the situation described on the card you've drawn. On the back write down one, two or three reasons why "you" (the person who caused the problem) might have acted the way you did. Write in the first person. ("I did it because _____.")

- When everyone has finished, each person reads both sides of his or her card out loud. Read the situation first and then the possible motivations you imagined.

- As you listen to the others, consider the motivations that were suggested for the person who hurt you. Are they feasible? Can you think of better ones?

## *Before the Next Session*

There is a right way and a wrong way to ask for forgiveness. Try saying these two sentences out loud and see which is more difficult:

> *1. I'm sorry.*
> *2. Will you forgive me?*

The hardest words in the world to say are "Will you forgive me?" It isn't enough to say "I'm sorry." That allows you to remain in control. Asking for forgiveness gives the offended person control over the decision, something human beings hate above almost anything else. It is also important to specifically acknowledge our offense when asking for forgiveness. (If we have cheated or stolen from someone, making restitution is essential.)

> *"I was wrong for judging the way you dress. Will you forgive me?"*
> *"I was wrong to betray your trust. Will you forgive me?"*
> *"I was wrong to lie to you. Will you forgive me?"*

The most freeing words in the world are "I was wrong," followed by "Will you forgive me?" They are freeing to the one saying them, and freeing to the one hearing them.

Try to forgive someone for something at least once this week.

# Session Nine
# Happiness

## Reflection

No one can guarantee happiness for someone else, and no one can expect to be happy all the time. Yet some happiness is necessary for every human being to survive. For us divorced people, however, the "Eleventh Commandment" seems to be *"Thou shalt be unhappy all the time."* For how can we think about happiness when we are so hurt, angry, afraid and frustrated?

We are told we won't find happiness by retreating into our memories, but neither can we be expected to passively suffer in silence while waiting for a brighter tomorrow. It's unrealistic to expect those of us in the grieving stage of divorce to always keep a smile plastered on our face. On the other hand, we will soon lose friends if we constantly take out our negative feelings on others.

Looking around at other people, we realize that their happiness does not depend on external situations, conditions or possessions. Surprisingly enough, many of them endure real suffering and hardship yet remain content and pleasant. Perhaps even more difficult to comprehend, some of those who seem to have the best of everything are still dissatisfied and unhappy.

It becomes evident that happiness depends in large part on how we react to our experiences and how we interpret the things that happen to us. It follows that if we can change our perceptions, we can go a long way toward changing our feelings. Developing a positive perspective on life may sound difficult for those of us in crisis situations, including divorce, but doing so is essential if we don't want to be controlled by every harsh wind that blows our way.

If happiness grows out of a vision of life, what perspective can help make us happy in unhappy circumstances? The New Testament teaches that God understands the human condition and wants us to find and fulfill ourselves in our pain and defeats as well as our joys and achievements. We are called to trust in the goodness of God, of others, of ourselves. We give hope by responding to the needs of others. We find our happiness not in isolation but through the things we do every day with and for others in our search for love and friendship. To be involved in something worthwhile and to love and be loved are the elements of real happiness. Making the pain of today an opportunity for growth, rather than a source of defeat, is one of the challenges that Christian living offers.

It's hard to find happiness when we are suffering. It won't come by itself. We must choose to be happy, learn how to be happy, and put in the necessary time, prayer and practice to be happy.

In *Psycho-Cybernetics*, Maxwell Maitz offers these insights into developing the "habit of happiness":

- To pursue happiness is to pursue a good; it is not a selfish occupation. On the contrary, it pulls us away from a self-centered preoccupation with our faults, sins and troubles. Looking outward opens us up to expressing ourselves creatively in helping others (the Christian formula for self-fulfillment).
- Happiness lies in the present. It isn't supposed to be deferred until a "better" time. You can't wait until all your problems have been solved before being happy. If you are to be happy at all, you must be "happy, period," not "happy because of...."
- Happiness is a mental habit that can be cultivated. It is produced by ideas and attitudes, which can be developed by your own activities, regardless of your environment. Abraham Lincoln once said, "Most people are about as happy as they make up their minds to be." Grumpiness, dissatisfaction, resentment and irritability are learned reactions to petty annoyances and frustrations. They have been practiced so often they've become habits. These habitual reactions largely originated in events that were interpreted as blows to self-esteem.
- Robert Louis Stevenson said, "The habit of being happy enables one to be freed, or largely freed, from the domination of outward conditions." It is a decision you make. You have the freedom to respond to events as you choose instead of according to the expectations of others. You can even improve your divorce situation and worries it causes by choosing not to add resentment and self-pity to your problems.
- People are goal-strivers. Reaching for goals adds to our sense of happiness and well-being. Positive, imaginative action is one way to overcome barriers to these goals. Running from these barriers means abandoning the goals.
- *Habit* originally meant "garment." Our habits are the garments our

personalities wear. We wear them because they fit our self-image and blend into our entire personality pattern. About 95 percent of our behavior is habitual. Our attitudes, emotions and beliefs tend to become habitual also. We tend to think, feel and act in the ways we learned were "appropriate." Nevertheless, we can modify or even reverse habits by making a conscious decision to do so and acting out the new responses or behavior. The key to changing habits is persistence and practice until the new behavior pattern comes to us as easily as the old habits did.

### Exercise One
*Write your responses in your notebook.*

1. Happiness is....
2. I am happy when....
3. I could be happy if....
4. I deserve to be happy because....

### Exercise Two
*Write your responses in your notebook.*

1. Happiness isn't always an intense "high" or even a long, warm glow. Each of us finds happiness in different sources, and we all experience it in different ways. List some of the things that make you happy, however small they may seem. Don't try to think too deeply about your answers. Just write the first things that come to mind.
2. "To be involved in something worthwhile and to love and be loved are the elements of real happiness." How do you feel about this statement?
3. In your particular situation, what do you think about "learning" how to be happy? Is it necessary, possible, desirable?
4. Name one or two things you can do in the next week to start developing the habit of happiness.

### Before the Next Session
Try to read this list every day and consciously follow as many of the statements as possible. After 21 days of practicing this discipline, your

worry, guilt and hostility should diminish and your confidence will increase. You might want to tape the list to your mirror, computer screen or refrigerator as a reminder.

- I will be as cheerful as possible.
- I will try to feel and act a little more friendly toward other people.
- I am going to be a little less critical and a little more tolerant of other people, especially of their faults, failings and mistakes. I will interpret their actions in the most favorable way possible.
- I am going to act as if success is inevitable and I already have the personality I want. I will practice "acting out" and "feeling like" this new personality.
- I will not let my opinion color facts in a pessimistic or negative way.
- I will practice smiling at least three times during the day.
- I will react as calmly and as intelligently as possible.
- I will not dwell on negative "facts" that I cannot change.

---

**Note**: *Decorate a shoebox and find a photo of your wedding day. You will use them for one of the Divorce Completion Rituals after Session Ten.*

---

# Session Ten
# Pathways to Growth

**Before We Begin**

At the beginning of the first session, you wrote your answers to three questions and put them in an envelope. Open your envelope and read your responses. Jot down any notes or observations you have as you read them. Take a few minutes to share your observations with one another.

## Reflection

This is the last session in the *Divorce and Beyond* program. It does not mean that you are completely recovered from your divorce or that you will now stop working on your own growth. It does mean that you are coming to the end of the "mourning period" of the divorce process. Soon, if not already, you will experience the gut feeling that—despite surges of nostalgia and resentment—the past no longer dominates your present. In *Creative Divorce,* Mel Krantzler offers these clues to help you recognize when this is true:

- Resentment and bitterness toward your former mate have subsided from a 24-hour obsession to occasional flashes of anger.
- You spend less time complaining about problems and more time trying to solve them.
- You begin calling old friends and making new friends, recognizing that you have no reason to be ashamed.
- You begin making decisions based on your interests and pleasures—taking a course, attending a play, entertaining friends.
- You no longer stereotype the opposite sex as threatening or despicable, and statements lumping all men or women together no longer seem accurate to you.
- You realize you are not the only person ever to have been divorced, that other normal people have ended unhappy marriages.
- You come to accept your divorce as the only realistic solution to a destructive marriage and not as a punishment for having failed.

If people lived in a storybook world, or if their lives could be programmed to follow a logical progression, we'd all pause right here and wait until everyone could truly say they were through mourning the death of their marriage and could go freely into the future. Unfortunately, the process isn't that neat and clean for most people. Life seldom gives us enough time and space to solve one problem before others appear. We divorced people are no exception to this. While still trying to let go of one life, we are forced to live daily in a new role. One way of smoothing things out, however, is to begin to do some interim planning now and establish some priorities and goals for ourselves.

Maybe setting goals seems unthinkable for you right now—something to do in the faraway future when all the "real" problems have been solved. But the future is tomorrow; the new you is here and already changing day by day. Happiness and security are real and attainable. No one can predict what tomorrow will bring, but those of us who can project our hopes and speculate on the possibilities for the future are usually more realistic. We are more flexible and better able to adapt to unusual events than those for whom every new experience is a shock or surprise.

Your first goal must be the acceptance of your new life as a single person. In his book *Growing Through Divorce*, Jim Smoke offers these insights and suggestions for reaching this goal:

- The longer you live in your identity as a married person, the longer you will block your potential for new growth. You are no longer married, so don't try to play the role.
- Though other people may wish to superimpose an identity on you, and although it might seem easier to become what other people want you to be, form your own identity. You are *you*, not what someone else thinks you are.
- You have a new role, so learn how to live it. Your new role will enable you to confront your identity problems in concrete, meaningful ways by challenging you to become a resourceful, independent single person and perhaps a single parent and maybe even a noncustodial parent.
- Realize that you are unique, an unrepeatable miracle of God. Develop a relationship with God to give you a foundation for your new identity.
- Though it is easy to dwell on and relive your old experiences, create new experiences to help you become an adventurer in the present rather than tenant of the past.

- Know that you have the freedom to fail. Human beings make mistakes. Take some risks. When you make mistakes, learn from them.

### Exercise
*Write your responses in your notebook.*

1. What one thing do you think you could do in the immediate future to help bring your "mourning period" to a close?
2. Write down and share with your group the first things that come to mind, positive or negative, when you think about rebuilding a new life. Don't try to sort out or censor your thoughts. Just let the words, phrases or images flow.
3. What feelings, thoughts or images about your new identity seem strongest to you right now?
4. Share with your group the most important thing you've learned through these sessions.

### During the Coming Weeks
Now is the best time to begin the last chapter in the "story" you started at the beginning of the program. Take some time, look at your expectations and limitations honestly, and set some goals. Jot down short sentences or phrases describing some features of your life as you'd like it to be three months from now, one year from now, and three years from now. To stimulate your imagination, describe each of these stages as it relates to such things as children, career, housing, and community and religious involvement.

Here are some suggestions to help you set and realize your goals:

1. List all the things you want out of life. Ask yourself these questions about the things on your list:
   - Is this really *my* goal?
   - Am I too afraid of past experiences to give it a fair try?
   - How will I know when I have reached my goal?
   - Is the goal worth the struggle?
   - Is the goal realistic, given my schedule, finances and talents as well as possible opposition from others?
2. Organize your goals in order of importance.
3. Work out specific things you can do to achieve each of your goals. Talk with others, and don't be afraid to ask for help.

4. Choose goals you can start working on immediately and that are short-term enough that you can achieve them easily. Some more ambitious goals may have to wait for a while to be attained.
5. Make sure your goals are clear, specific, measurable and realistic.

---

### Self-Affirmation and Stress

Keep up with whatever practices in this book have worked well for you. When you feel you have mastered one thing to the point that it has become a habit, try another. Develop your own program of relaxation and self-affirmation. Only you can provide the time, effort, information, determination and patience required to bring forth the masterpiece that is the real you.

---

# Creating a New Vocabulary

After a divorce you will find it necessary to amend many basic words and concepts about family. For example, your *home* is no longer a place that houses a husband and wife or a mother, father and children. Christmas is no longer a holiday during which you all celebrate together all the old cherished rituals.

Comparing your current situation with your previous one may create frustration or depression. It is important, therefore, to form new verbal associations for some of your familiar concepts. After all, marriage is not a part of every family. Now that you are divorced, you still have a home and rituals, and your children may have two homes and two sets of rituals.

One way to break free from old associations is to build a new vocabulary. Words mold your thinking. Pay particular attention to language that describes your status, your self-esteem, and your accomplishments.

The first and perhaps hardest vocabulary change is to start referring to yourself as "I" rather than "we," as in "my spouse and I." More generally, replace unpleasant, negative or defensive words with words that indicate satisfaction, confidence and a sense of pride.

In *Mom's House, Dad's House,* Isolina Ricci offers these guidelines:

- Weed out negative or unrealistic beliefs and establish your own meaning for the words *family, home* and *parenthood.*
- Separate your role as a former spouse from that as a single person and perhaps single parent.
- Set up your new home (or reorganize the old one, if necessary) and establish your own family rituals, customs and rules.
- Finally, when confronted with certain situations, consider the vocabulary changes on the following page.

| Instead of saying | Try saying |
| --- | --- |
| Motherless, fatherless, split or broken home | Our home |
| Wife, husband, spouse (ex-wife, ex-husband) | Former spouse |
| Custodial parent, non-custodial parent | Children's mother, children's father |
| Remarriage, reconstituted family, blended family, combination family | Our family, our new family |
| I have children, but they live with their (father or mother) | I have a family. |
| The children are visiting. their (mom or dad) | The children are at their (mom's or dad's) house. |
| The children have one home. Their (mother or father) visits. | The children have two homes. They live at both. |
| The marriage broke up or failed. | The marriage ended. |

# Program Completion Rituals

**Note**: *These may be done immediately after Session Ten or at a separate gathering. They may be done at the regular meeting place or in a church or chapel.*

## Ritual One
## Accepting Where We Are

### Materials
Soft, meditative music
A candle and matches
A baggie for each person containing a pen, one piece of 15-inch wired ribbon, one small stone, and two index cards
Each person brings a decorated and personalized shoebox
Each person brings a wedding photo

### Ceremony

*Light the candle. Play music as people gather and get settled.*
*Each participant holds his or her shoebox, baggie of materials, and pen.*

**Reader:**  For everything there is a season,
and a time for every matter under heaven:
A time to be born, and a time to die;
A time to plant, and a time to pluck up what is planted,
A time to kill, a time to heal;
A time to break down, and a time to build up.
A time to weep, and a time to laugh.
*Ecclesiastes 3:1-4*

**Leader**: When you married, divorce was not part of the plan for your life. Our group has attempted to help each of us center ourselves and try to put his or her divorce in its proper perspective and move on. Those words were easy to say, but the feelings are difficult to make

71

real. This ceremony is to help us bring these sessions to a conclusion. It celebrates a new beginning, not an end.

Take an index card and write today's date. Think of where you were when you started this program, and where you are today. Put the date card in the box.

On the second index card, write the two worst things about being divorced, what you hate the most.

Take this card and crumple it up. Notice that the card does not crumple easily; your feelings are so strong.

Now put it in the box.

Pick up your stone. Hold it in your hand, feel it. It is solid but not smooth. This stone symbolizes your life after your divorce: strong and solid, yet shaped by what you have weathered. Put the stone in the box.

Take your wedding photo. Most likely you were once happy and excited about your former spouse. Close your eyes for a minute and picture one very good time you had together. Look at the picture and think of something good about your marriage. Put the photo in the box.

Now take the piece of ribbon. Tie it into a bow. Think of how close you once felt to your former spouse. Look at the bow, knotted in the middle.

Take each end of the ribbon and gently tug. The bow is coming undone; the knot separates. Look at the ribbon. It is not a fancy bow any more, just a plain ribbon, but it is strong on its own. It is strong enough to be reshaped in the future.

Smooth out the ribbon and put it in the box.


**Reader**:      For everything, there is a season,
And a time for every matter under heaven....
A time to mourn, and a time to dance;
A time to throw away stones, and a time to gather stones together.
A time to embrace, and a time to refrain from embracing;
A time to seek, and a time to lose;
A time to keep, and a time to throw away...
A time to keep silent, and a time to speak.
A time to love, and a time to hate;
A time for war, and a time for peace.
*Ecclesiastes 3:1, 4-8*


**Leader**: For weeks you have wrestled with your divorce journey. While you are not finished, you have made a start. Slowly put the cover on your box. When you go home, you may want to add other significant items to this box. Then put it away, but do not throw it out. Put it wherever you feel comfortable with it—on your dresser, in the attic, in the corner of a dark closet. Someday you may need to take it out and remember the grace you received during this session.

Everything takes time. We trust that God will give us the strength we need.

**All:**                    **The Serenity Prayer**
God, grant me the serenity
To accept the things I cannot change,
the courage to change the things I can,
and the wisdom to know the difference.
Living one day at a time,
Enjoying one moment at a time,
Accepting hardship as the pathway to peace.
Taking, as he did, this sinful world as it is, not as I would have it.
Trusting that he will make all things right if I surrender to his will.
That I may be reasonably happy in this life,
And supremely happy with him forever in the next.
Amen.

# Ritual Two
# Heeding the Call to Growth

## Materials
Recording of "Abba Father"
One golf-ball-sized piece of soft clay (the kind that never dries to hardness) for each person

## Ceremony

*Play "Abba Father" softly as people gather.*

**Leader**: We are forever being formed. We never remain quite the same. Our joys and our sorrows mold us and shape us. And so we ask for the capacity to use our sufferings in such a way that we are forever open to becoming the complete person God has in mind for us.

**All**: May the God of strength be with us and keep us in strong-fingered hands. May we be a sacrament of strength to those we meet. May the God of wonder be with us, delighting us with thunder and wind, sunrise and rain, enchanting our senses, filling our hearts, and opening our eyes to the splendor of his creation. May the God of patience be with us, waiting for us with outstretched arms, letting us find out for ourselves. May the God of peace be with us, stilling the heart that hammers with fear, doubt and confusion. And may the warm mantle of God's peace cover our anxiety.

**Leader**: We do not shape God; God shapes us. If we are to be the work of God, we need to await the hand of the artist who does all things in due season. As St. Irenaeus said, "Let your clay be moist, lest you grow hard and lose the imprint of God's fingers."

**Reader 1:** The Lord said to me, "Go down to the potter's house, where I will give you my message." So I went there and saw the potter working at his wheel. Whenever a piece of pottery turned out imperfectly, he would take the clay and make it into something else.
*Jeremiah 18:1-4*

**Reader 2:** Then the Lord said to me: "Don't I have the right to do with you people of Israel what the potter did with the clay? You are in my hands just like clay in the potter's hands. If at any time I say that I am going to uproot, break down or destroy any nation or kingdom, but then the nation turns from its evil, I will not do what I said I would. On the other hand, if I say that I am going to plant or build up any nation or kingdom, but then that nation disobeys me and does evil, I will not do what I said I would.... Don't I have the right to do to you people of Israel what the potter did with the clay?"

*Jeremiah 18:5-10*

**Reader 3:** Just as clay is in the potter's hands for him to shape as he pleases, so we are in the hands of our Creator for him to do with as he wishes.

*Sirach 33:13*

**Leader**: What is it that you want God to shape in you? Please take a moment to shape your piece of clay into something that represents how you want God to shape you.

*(Take time to allow all to share what they tried to symbolize with their clay and how it made them feel. "Abba Father" plays softly while people work. Allow 3 to 5 minutes.)*

**Leader**: May the God of love be with us, drawing us close.

**All**: May God's love in us be for those we meet; may this love in us glow in our eyes and reflect the love in the eyes of our family and friends; may we share this love with all those who find themselves in need.

**Leader**: May we always be open and pliant to what God wants of us. May we always be ready to allow the Divine Potter to gently shape us. Amen.

# The Catholic Annulment Process

*Is an annulment a "Catholic divorce"?*
*What is an annulment?*
*Does it cost a fortune to get an annulment?*
*How can a long-term marriage be annulled?*
*Will the children be illegitimate if an annulment is granted?*
*Why would anyone want an annulment?*

There are many misconceptions about the annulment process in the Catholic Church. The popular media do not thoroughly report Church teaching on this touchy issue. Often, family elders are the ones sought out for information about annulment. But they are not necessarily updated on Church teaching and tell family members what they know based on what they were taught decades ago. Many divorced people wonder what the facts are about the process. They often don't even know where to go to learn about it.

## What is an Annulment?

Let's start with first things first. The Church officially uses the term "declaration of nullity" rather than "annulment," although here we will use the popular term. An annulment is a declaration by a competent Church authority that a marriage that appeared to be binding and valid was in fact neither binding nor valid from the beginning; that is, some essential element was missing.

The Tribunal arrives at such a conclusion only after it has investigated the marriage and the circumstances surrounding its beginnings. An annulment is radically different from a civil divorce, which can be obtained for serious or less-than-serious reasons. The Tribunal is concerned with a person's intentions, knowledge and ability to make a lifelong commitment at the time of the marriage ceremony itself.

A declaration of nullity by the Church is not made easily. However, particularly in American culture, essential elements of a sacramental marriage are often missing at the time a couple exchanges their consent. For example: A young woman marries to escape an abusive home. She later sees that her husband is an alcoholic. There may even be proof of domestic violence in her own marriage. Upon investigation, the Tribunal finds that she demonstrated a lack of mature judgment when she chose to marry in the first place. This information gives the Tribunal grounds to declare the marriage null from the beginning, thereby granting an "annulment."

There are many other situations and sets of circumstances that can lead to an annulment. In long-term marriages it is more difficult to grant a declaration of nullity, but it is possible and does occur.

The Church has a long tradition of insisting on the indissolubility of marriage. One man and one woman—for life—is the teaching that Jesus proposed and that the Church has echoed throughout the centuries. Divorce with the right to remarry has not been part of our Catholic tradition, and the Sacrament of Matrimony is held in high regard in our faith tradition. When a couple marries, the Church assumes that marriage to be binding and valid until proven otherwise.

On the other hand, if married life causes harm of body or spirit to either person, the couple does not have to continue living together. Many divorced couples never should have married in the first place. Therefore, it is important to look at the capacity of the couple—at the time they exchanged their vows—if their union is to be considered a "sacramental marriage" as defined by the Church. Upon investigation, it is not at all unusual to find some essential element missing in one or both parties at the time their marital consent was exchanged. This does not mean that they did not intend to get married, but it does mean that they were *incapable* of making a sacramental commitment at the time.

This Church annulment process has no *legal* implications whatsoever. In fact, a couple cannot apply for an annulment until after a legal divorce has already happened. Nor does an annulment deny legitimacy to any children they have or waive responsibility for child support. Church law affirms the legitimacy of the children and reminds both parents that they have rights and responsibilities regarding their children. An annulment does not say the couple was never married. Of course they were married, but not as the Church defines the sacrament of marriage.

## How Does an Annulment Work?

Anyone whose marriage has failed and has ended in a civil divorce may approach the Church and ask for an investigation to determine whether or not the marriage was valid according to Church law. The person seeking the annulment is called the "petitioner." In most dioceses, the petitioner begins by visiting a priest, deacon or other parish minister. With that person's help, an initial application is filled out asking the diocesan Tribunal to begin an investigation. After the ap-

78

plication is submitted, a questionnaire and/or personal interview is required of the petitioner to determine additional details about what caused the marriage to break down. It does not really matter how long the marriage lasted; however, the Tribunal usually seeks more evidence to establish the nullity of a long-term marriage than it does for one that lasted only a short time.

### What About the Cost?
It is easy to get the impression from the media that annulments are primarily for the rich or famous. Headlines are often made when a public figure is granted an annulment from the Church and the hurting and often publicly-jilted former spouse talks to the press. We rarely hear from the thousands of ordinary Catholics who have benefited greatly from an annulment about the particulars of the process.

It does cost money to run a Tribunal with the requisite support staff. Employees of the Tribunal are paid salaries and benefits to support themselves and their families. The annulment petitioner is asked to absorb some—but definitely not all—of that cost. Each diocese has a different fee structure depending on the size of the diocese and the workload of the Tribunal. The cost a petitioner is asked to pay is usually more than $200 and less than $1,000, but no one is denied access to the annulment process for financial reasons. Fees are waived or reduced if necessary.

### How Long Does It Take to Get an Annulment?
There are horror stories about how long the annulment process takes to complete. When the petitioner follows the procedures in a timely and conscientious manner, however, the process is rather efficient. The case does not open until the petitioner's "story," or testimony, is submitted to the Tribunal and a judge is assigned the case. Depending on the volume of cases and the size of the Tribunal staff, it can take one to two years to decide a case once it is assigned to a judge.

Many people enter the annulment process in order to get answers for themselves as to what really happened in their marriage that led to the divorce. Others seek a divorce because they have met (or hope to meet) someone they would like to marry in the Church. It is a good idea to consider seeking an annulment a few months after your civil divorce is completed. By then your legal proceedings should be over, yet the facts of your marriage and divorce are still fresh in your mind. The annulment process will provide you the opportunity to take a good hard look at your marriage though the eyes of the Church and then retire it to a place other than the forefront of your mind.

## Is the Annulment Process Painful or Difficult?

The annulment process does require that you look at your marriage once again, and some say that just as the wound from your marriage is finally healing you are asked to pry the scab off the wound and look under it. But the purpose of the annulment process is not to reopen old wounds but to heal them once and for all. In telling your story, you must review your background, the background of your former spouse, and the marriage itself. It requires digging up old memories, recalling things you have tried hard to forget. It can be painful and difficult. However, facing the facts of a failed marriage and dredging up the hurt and rejection one last time can aid in the healing process.

Through the annulment process, you can come to a deeper self-knowledge, so that mistakes of the past will not be repeated (whether you ever remarry or not). God and the Church know that people who have been through a divorce have already suffered tremendously. The storytelling in your testimony and your conversations with Tribunal staff are designed to get at the truth and help you to heal. Once an annulment is granted, it gives you freedom to marry again in the Catholic Church, should you ever wish to do so.

## What if an Application for an Annulment Is Turned Down?

A difficult and painful reality of the process is that sometimes an annulment is not granted. In these cases you have four choices:

- You can reapply using different grounds. This will require additional proof and witnesses, and you will need to retell the story of your marriage. It is the same process as before, looked at through a different lens.
- You can ask the Vatican to investigate the denial of your original application. Generally it takes years to get an answer this way.
- You can accept the decision and move on, recognizing that you are not free to marry again in the Church. It must be emphasized that divorced people, even without an annulment, are still welcome to attend Mass and receive the sacraments as long as they do not remarry outside the Church.
- You can deal with your situation in what is called the "internal forum." This means that you resolve the issue privately following your own informed conscience under the spiritual direction of a priest. The decision to use the internal forum should be arrived at only after an application for a declaration of nullity has been officially turned down. An internal forum is not publicly recorded or recognized. It is a private matter between you and God.

## Future Marriage

Some who have received annulments take the awareness they gain in the annulment process and use it to develop a solid relationship with another person and decide to marry again in the Church. Likewise, those who married outside the Church after a divorce and now have received an annulment approach the Church for "convalidation" of their current marriage. Some people call this "blessing" a second marriage, but what we are actually celebrating is the Sacrament of Matrimony between a couple who are now free to marry in the eyes of the Church.

The Church wants second marriages to be healthy and happy, and so sometimes counseling is recommended before the Church allows another marriage, even after an annulment has been granted. This is not meant to be a reflection on a past marriage or the psychological health of either person in a proposed new one. Rather, it is a safeguard for the future to help ensure that a couple is prepared to manage issues from the past in a new marriage. "To be forewarned is to be forearmed," as they say@

## Healing and Hope

Going through the annulment process can teach us the deep meaning behind being married in the Church. Many people say during work on an annulment that they wish they had this knowledge before they married the first time. How true! The annulment process can teach us to manage the pain of loss. We may not get all of our questions answered, but we can heal some of the bitterness and hurt that is part of every divorce. An annulment can provide hope for a better tomorrow. It can help us regain self-respect lost in the trauma of divorce. And it can help us close the door on a painful chapter of our life and open the door to a better future.

Just as there are no easy divorces, there are no easy annulments. Each one takes time and effort. Remember the story of Jesus and the woman at the well. He forgave her, and she drank the "living water" when he invited her to do so. Like the woman at the well, we can drink of the hope, healing and understanding the annulment process can provide.

---

**Note**: For further information on the Catholic annulment process, including sample responses to the questions asked, see the book *Annulment: A Step-by-Step Guide for Divorced Catholics* by Fr. Ronald Smith (ACTA Publications, 1995).

---

# Additional Resources

## Books

*Catholics Experiencing Divorce: Grieving, Healing and Learning to Live Again,* Rev. William E. Rabior, ACSW, and Vicki Wells Bedard (Ligouri Publications, 1991)

*Catholics, Marriage and Divorce: Real People, Real Questions,* Victoria Vonderberger, RSM (St. Anthony Messenger Press, 2004)

*Design For Wholeness: Dealing With Anger, Learning To Forgive, Building Self-Esteem,* Loughlan Sofield, ST, Carroll Juliano, SHCJ, and Rosine Hammett, CSC (Ave Maria Press, 1990)

*Growing Through Divorce,* Jim Smoke (Harvest House Publishers, 1995)

*Moving Forward: A Devotional Guide for Finding Hope and Peace in the Midst of Divorce,* Jim Smoke (Hendrickson Publishers, 2000)

*The New Day Journal,* Mauryeen O'Brien, OP (ACTA Publications, 2000)

*Praying Through Your Divorce,* Karen O'Donnell (St. Anthony Messenger Press, 2003)

*The Return of the Prodigal Son: A Story of Homecoming,* Rev. Henri J.M. Nouwen (Doubleday, 1992)

*Should I Stay or Go? How Controlled Separation Can Save Your Marriage,* Lee Raffel, MSW (Contemporary Books, 1999)

*Tear Soup: A Recipe for Healing After Loss,* Pat Schweibert and Chuck DeKlyen, illustrated by Taylor Bills (Grief Watch/ACTA Publications, 1999)

*Traits of a Healthy Spirituality,* Melannie Svoboda, SND (Twenty-Third Publications, 1996)

*The Unexpected Legacy of Divorce: A 25 Year Landmark Study,* Judith A. Wallerstein, Julia M. Lewis and Sandra Blakeslee (Hyperion, 2000)

*You Give Them Something to Eat: Ministering When You Think You Can't,* Joe Paprocki (Ave Maria Press, 1998)

## Internet

www.divorcecare.org
www.divorcemagazine.com
www.divorcerecovery101.com

www.divorcesupport.com
www.familyministries.org/divorce.htm
www.nacsdc.org
www.rainbows.org
www.smartmarriages.com

## Videos

*Shattered Dreams: Healing After Divorce* (Paraclete Press, 2002)

*Raising Children of Divorce: Practical Help for Parents* (Paraclete Press, 2002)

*Dream's End: Spiritual Recovery from Divorce and Separation* (Oblate Media and Communications Corp., 1995)

*Children of Divorce* (PBS, 2000)

*The American Family: A Challenged Tradition-Rebuilding After Divorce* (Notre Dame Alumni Continuing Education and Golden Dome Productions, 1997)

## Other

*Divorce and Beyond Facilitators Guide,* Elsie P. Radtke (ACTA Publications, 2004)

*Relationship Enlightenment Facilitator Guide, Desiree and Tom Marciani* (Family Life Office, Diocese of Joliet, 2000)

"Disentwining Souls: What Catholics Can Learn from Jewish Divorce," Jennifer Paquette, *U.S. Catholic,* December 2002, p. 38

# Acknowledgments

Since the original publication of this book in 1983, the wisdom and compassion of the authors, James Greteman and Leon Haverkamp, has helped many people. This new edition has been updated to incorporate current research and teaching, and it gives the book a more contemporary look.

This edition has been influenced by people all over the United States. All of the people who have made contributions to it have either worked with this book in divorce support ministries or have benefited from it in their own divorce recovery process. To all of them I give a heartfelt thank you.

The North American Conference of Separated and Divorced Catholics (NACSDC) has encouraged this work. Irene Varley, the executive director, contributed the Foreword. Bob Zulinski, the president, gave me copious comments and suggestions, most of which I incorporated.

Kim Hagerty, ministry coordinator for the Family Ministries Office of the Archdiocese of Chicago, wrote one of the ritual services and proofread the first draft. Brother Ken Pinc, OSF, coordinator of the Family Ministries office of the Archdiocese of Indianapolis, wrote the second ritual. Louise Ritz, director of the Family Life office for the Diocese of Pensacola-Tallahassee (Florida), helped form the criteria for selecting good ministers to lead the recovery process using this book. Desiree and Tom Marciani offered their Relationship Enlightenment program to enrich the session on forgiveness. Desiree is the associate director of the Family Life Office for the Diocese of Joliet (Illinois), and Tom is studying to be a deacon in that diocese. Frank Hannigan, director of the Family Ministries Office of the Archdiocese of Chicago, allowed me the time to revise this book to enhance the Christian outreach to those affected by divorce.

Recovery from the trauma of divorce is not done alone. The *Divorce and Beyond* program is meant to be shared with others going through similar loss. I first realized in a meeting years ago that for me God becomes evident when I hear others speak of their pain and loss. It is in listening to other people as they reveal their humanness that God is clearly in our midst. Watch for it and you will see it, too.

People often tell me their Church turned its back on them at the time of their divorce. Churches are buildings and cannot turn at all. It is the responsibility of each person to reach out and begin their healing process with the help and support of others on this journey of divorce recovery. *Divorce and Beyond* gives divorced and divorcing people that opportunity.

Thank you to all those mentioned here and those who have used this resource for the past 20 years. May God bless all you new readers as you use this book in your divorce recovery. Your journey toward healing has begun.

# *Prayers for Those Experiencing Divorce*

## Between Dust and Angelhood

Dear God,
    your Bible says it well:
    what a work we humans are!

In one sense: "mere dust of the earth;"
    in another: "little less than the angels."

At times, God,
    |I feel that pull inside
    between dust and angelhood.

Help me to grow in self-knowledge
    by giving me the courage to look inside.

May I have a healthy self-esteem,
    one that steers clear
    of demonic despair
    and Pharisaic pride.

May I never identify solely with innocence;
Rather, help me to know my sins and failings,
    while never doubting
    the flow of your mercy.

God, source of all esteem,
    help me to say each day,
    "I'm happy I'm me."

And to hear you reply,
    "Me too!"

Amen.

*M. Svoboda*

## A Prayer about Anger

Anger is a part of my life, Lord. I don't understand it and I don't like it, but it's there. Sometimes I am just tired. Sometimes I'm upset with myself. Most often I'm just too involved figuring out my own thing to care about others. And away it goes. I blow my top, let off steam, and take it out on others.

Is anger good and bad, Lord? I know you chased the money people out of the temple. And you showed your displeasure with disciples who kept children from you. Can anger be okay for human beings too?

If I don't let my anger out, it bottles up, Lord. Is that worse than letting it come? Help me admit to my angry feelings. Lead me to friends who can help me turn anger into something good for others and myself. Remind me that you also love and accept people who get angry.

Amen.

*E. Witt*

# On Being Me

Let my entire person reflect my relationship to you, dear Lord.

Help me not to be afraid of being myself.
Enable me to be who I am and all that I am.
Let me escape Me the trap of comparisons,
Through your patience and love.

> Help me accept others
> Who are like me
> Or very different from me
> And remember that it's okay
> For them to be who they are,
> Through your patience and love.

There's so much more to me
Than physical appearance
And clothes
And how I wear my hair
And the music I like.
Help me like the me I am,
Through your patience and love.

> Live within me
> And give me confidence
> So I can live honestly
> With my family, friends
> And with myself,
> Through your patience and love.

Amen.

*adapted from E. Witt*

## Loneliness

Loneliness means walls, Lord,
Between me and everyone.

Help me see freedom
as the opposite of loneliness
and doors instead of walls
and everyone else as
confused by me as I am by them.

Open my doors to freedom, Lord.
Surround me with real people,
with love that lasts
and hope that keeps coming back.
Like You, Lord.

Amen.

*E. Witt*

## Prayer for the Divorced

God, master of union and disunion,
Teach me how I may now walk
Alone and strong.

Heal my wounds;
Let the scar tissue of thy bounty
Cover these hurts and bruises
That I may again be a single person
Adjusted to new days.

Grant me a heart of wisdom,
Cleanse me of hostility, revenge and rancor.
Make me know the laughter which is not giddy,
The affection which is not frightened.

Keep far from me thoughts of evil and despair.
May I realize that the past chapter of my life has changed,
The expected story end will not come.

Shall I mourn at the turn of the plot?
Rather, remembering without anger's thrust,
Recalling without repetitive pain of regret,
Teach me again to write and read
That I may convert this unexpected epilogue
Into a new preface and a new poem.

Muddled gloom over,
Tension days passed,
Let bitterness of thought fade,
Harshness of memory attenuate.

Make me move on in love and kindness.

*M. Fisher*

## Slow Me Down, Lord

Give me, amid the confusion of the day,
    the calmness of the everlasting hills.
Break the tensions
of my nerves and muscles with the soothing music
of the singing streams that live in my memory.

Help me to know the magical
    restoring power of sleep.

Teach me the art of making minute vacations—
    of slowing down to look at a flower,
    to chat with a friend, to pat a dog,
    to read a few lines from a good book.

Slow me down, Lord, and inspire me to send
    my roots deep into the soil of life's enduring
    values, that I may grow towards the stars
    of my destiny.

Amen.

*R. Cushing*

## Additional Resources from ACTA Publications

*Hidden Presence*
*Twelve Blessings That Transformed Sorrow or Loss*
Edited by Gregory F. Augustine Pierce

A collection of true stories of blessings that somehow transformed a sorrow or loss. Each of the twelve storytellers in this book recalls a very real benefit or insight gained from a tragedy, failure, illness or disaster in his or her life. (176-page hardcover gift book with silver ribbon, $17.95)

*Tear Soup*
*A Recipe for Healing after Loss*
Pat Schwiebert and Chuck DeKlyen
Illustrated by Taylor Bills

This modern-day fable tells the story of a woman who has suffered a terrible loss and must cook up a special batch of "tear soup" in order to grieve. Richly illustrated, for children and adults alike. (56-page hardcover gift book, $19.95)

*From Grief to Grace*
*Images for Overcoming Sadness and Loss*
Helen R. Lambin

A collection of images that assist people in naming, processing and overcoming grief caused by divorce, illness, a loved one's death, a job loss or similar difficult situations. (96-page paperback, $8.95)

*Protect Us from All Anxiety*
*Meditations for the Depressed*
William Burke

A popular book for people suffering from serious depression, written by a priest of the Archdiocese of Chicago who suffers from depression himself. Provides insights into coping spiritually with the disease. (128-page paperback, $9.95)

**Available from booksellers or call 800-397-2282**
**www.actapublications.com**